"This is a *fantastic* volume. Shahar offers an accessible, compelling, and compact defense of the permissibility of eating meat—it's perfect for the classroom. At the same time, he's written a book that's full of material that pushes this important conversation forward. (His discussion of the Stag Hunt alone is worth the sticker price.) Whoever you are and whatever you make of his conclusions, Shahar's arguments are worth careful consideration."

— Bob Fischer, *Texas State University*

"Anyone asking themselves whether they should become a vegetarian will find this book to be an invaluable resource. For the difficult to balance criteria of accessibility and comprehensiveness, *Why It's OK to Eat Meat* is unsurpassed. To Shahar's credit, the issues are given such a balanced treatment that some readers will surely reach the opposite conclusion to the one expressed in the title."

— Paul B. Thompson, *Michigan State University*

"In the course of presenting state-of-the-art arguments that it's OK to eat meat, Shahar succeeds in getting us to focus on the bigger picture. What actions and attitudes actually help us advance justice and wellbeing? Which are just virtue-signaling sideshows? Vegetarians and meat-eaters alike owe it to us all to take these challenging questions seriously."

— Mark Budolfson, *Rutgers University*

Why It's OK
to Eat Meat

Vegetarians have argued at great length that meat-eating is wrong. Even so, the vast majority of people continue to eat meat, and even most vegetarians eventually give up on their diets. Does this prove these people must be morally corrupt?

In *Why It's OK to Eat Meat*, Dan C. Shahar argues the answer is no: it's entirely possible to be an ethical person while continuing to eat meat—and not just the "fancy" offerings from the farmers' market but also the regular meat we find at most supermarkets and restaurants. Shahar's examination forcefully echoes vegetarians' concerns about the meat industry's impacts on animals, workers, the environment, and public health. However, he shows that the most influential ethical arguments for avoiding meat on the basis of these considerations are ultimately unpersuasive. Instead of insisting we all become vegetarians, Shahar argues each of us has broad latitude to choose which of the world's problems to tackle, in what ways, and to what extents, and hence people can decline to take up this particular form of activism without doing anything wrong.

Dan C. Shahar is Assistant Professor of Philosophy—Research at the University of New Orleans and a member of the Urban Entrepreneurship and Policy Institute. He is the winner of the International Society for Environmental Ethics' 2020 Holmes Rolston III Early Career Essay Prize for Environmental Philosophy and co-editor (with David Schmidtz) of the latest edition of *Environmental Ethics: What Really Matters, What Really Works* (2018).

Why It's OK: The Ethics and Aesthetics of How We Live

Philosophers often build cogent arguments for unpopular positions. Recent examples include cases against marriage and pregnancy, for treating animals as our equals, and dismissing some popular art as aesthetically inferior. What philosophers have done less often is to offer compelling arguments for widespread and established human behavior, like getting married, having children, eating animals, and going to the movies. But if one role for philosophy is to help us reflect on our lives and build sound justifications for our beliefs and actions, it seems odd that philosophers would neglect arguments for the lifestyles most people—including many philosophers—actually lead. Unfortunately, philosophers' inattention to normalcy has meant that the ways of life that define our modern societies have gone largely without defense, even as whole literatures have emerged to condemn them.

Why It's OK: The Ethics and Aesthetics of How We Live seeks to remedy that. It's a series of books that provides accessible, sound, and often new and creative arguments for widespread ethical and aesthetic values. Made up of short volumes that assume no previous knowledge of philosophy from the reader, the series recognizes that philosophy is just as important for understanding what we already believe as it is for criticizing the status quo. The series isn't meant to make us complacent about what we value; rather, it helps and challenges us to think more deeply about the values that give our daily lives meaning.

Titles in Series:

Why It's OK to Want to Be Rich
Jason Brennan

Why It's OK to Be of Two Minds
Jennifer Church

Why It's OK to Ignore Politics
Christopher Freiman

Why It's OK to Make Bad Choices
William Glod

Why It's OK to Enjoy the Work of Immoral Artists
Mary Beth Willard

Why It's OK to Speak Your Mind
Hrishikesh Joshi

Why It's OK to Be a Slacker
Alison Suen

Selected Forthcoming Titles:

Why It's OK to Get Married
Christie J. Hartley

Why It's OK to Love Bad Movies
Matthew Strohl

Why It's OK to Mind Your Own Business
Justin Tosi and Brandon Warmke

Why It's OK to Be Fat
Rekha Nath

Why It's OK to Be a Socialist
Christine Sypnowich

For further information about this series, please visit: www.routledge.com/
Why-Its-OK/book-series/WIOK

DAN C. SHAHAR

Why It's OK
to Eat Meat

Routledge
Taylor & Francis Group
NEW YORK AND LONDON

First published 2022
by Routledge
605 Third Avenue, New York, NY 10158

and by Routledge
2 Park Square, Milton Park, Abingdon, Oxon, OX14 4RN

Routledge is an imprint of the Taylor & Francis Group, an informa business

Library of Congress Cataloging-in-Publication Data
A catalog record for this title has been requested

ISBN: 978-0-367-17275-6 (hbk)
ISBN: 978-0-367-17276-3 (pbk)
ISBN: 978-1-003-22194-4 (ebk)

DOI: 10.4324/9781003221944

Typeset in Joanna MT and DIN Pro
by SPi Technologies India Pvt Ltd (Straive)

Contents

Contents

So many people deserve thanks for helping this book come into being. My wife, Amy, was a tireless champion throughout the research and writing process, and my ability to deliver this manuscript to the publisher on time was due in no small part to her confidence, patience, and thoughtful comments. Both of our families have been tremendous sources of support as well—thanks especially to Mom, Dad, Lital, and Susan for everything that's gone into putting me in a position to complete a project like this.

I've been fortunate to draw on a wide network of incredible colleagues in the process of producing this book. Mark Budolfson, Bob Fischer, Siobhain Lash, JP Messina, Jake Monaghan, David O'Brien, Alexander Benzer Reid, Jeremy Reid, Lucy Schwarz, Chad Van Schoelandt, and an anonymous referee read the entire draft manuscript and provided extensive feedback. Cheryl Abbate, Brandon Ashby, Sameer Bajaj, Jacob Barrett, Geoff Brennan, Ray Cannata, Bryan Chambliss, Chelsea Crews, Crawford Crews, Jerry Gaus, Adam Gjesdal, Keith Hankins, Chris Howard, Audra Jenson, Caroline King, Brian Kogelmann, Will Leonard, Yael Loewenstein, Theresa Lopez, Doug MacLean, Lena Messina, Joe Metz, Tyler Millhouse, Brooke Monaghan, Francesco Nappo, Pavel Nitchovski, Nathan Oakes Joseph Porter, Z Quanbeck, Sarah Raskoff, Greg Robson, Geoff Sayre-McCord, Alex Schaefer, David Schmidtz, Rachel Schneebaum, Matt

Schuler, Paul Schwennesen, Chris Surprenant, Eyal Tal, John Thrasher, Hannah Tierney, Kevin Vallier, Alex von Stein, Sam Wakil, Steve Wall, Robert Wallace, and the participants in Eric Winsberg's spring 2021 environmental ethics course (including Eric) have been invaluable conversation partners on issues contained in this book and earlier work that helped inform it. (No doubt I've forgotten to mention numerous people from whom this project has benefited in important ways—I am sincerely sorry about that.)

For financial support during the process of writing this book, I am grateful to the John Templeton Foundation, the Institute for Humane Studies, and the Urban Entrepreneurship and Policy Institute at the University of New Orleans. The Institute for Humane Studies deserves special thanks for supporting a manuscript workshop in spring 2021 as part of the New Orleans Political Economy Roundtable. Thanks also to Andy Beck, Marc Stratton, Karthik Thiruvengadam, and Keith Povey for all their help with the practical aspects of getting this manuscript into print. This book wouldn't exist in a form you could read without all the hard work put in by Andy, Marc, Karthik, Keith, and countless others at Routledge and SPi Global, and it wouldn't exist at all if Andy hadn't reached out to me in the spring of 2018 to gauge my interest in writing it.

Finally, let me say thanks to you for your interest in this book. The issues we'll be discussing over the coming pages are important and challenging, and most people don't spare the time to think seriously about them. I don't take for granted the investment you're making in committing to read this volume. Here's hoping I do justice to the opportunity.

One

If you traveled back in time a few hundred years, what would people be eating? For the most part, the answer is: whatever they had. For almost all of human history, people weren't picky about their food. They couldn't afford to be. Culinary options were limited, and people ate what was available in order to survive.

Today, things are different. People in developed nations (i.e., virtually everyone reading this book) often attend closely to how food tastes, how healthy it is, how it was prepared, and where its ingredients came from, among many other factors. Unlike our ancestors (and unlike many people around the world today), we can choose what we eat, and that freedom has made it possible to be selective about what we put in our mouths.

Examining our diets often turns up unpleasant truths. Much of the food we eat is bad for us. Much of it is produced in ways that negatively impact the environment. Many of the people who work in the food sector are treated and paid badly. Particularly significantly for this book, most of the animals we eat are raised in poor conditions.

Problems like these pervade our food system, but they especially afflict the meat industry. Obviously, animal welfare issues fall distinctly into its lap. But the industry's activities also raise serious concerns about worker mistreatment,

DOI: 10.4324/9781003221944-1

environmental degradation, and public health endangerment, among many other things.

As awareness of these problems has spread, so too has a conviction that it's not just *unwise* to eat meat (e.g., for reasons of good health or frugality) but *morally wrong*. Globally, millions of people now describe themselves as "ethical vegetarians." The movement has grown substantially in recent decades, with many more people abstaining from meat today than was true when our parents and grandparents were raised.[1]

The purpose of this book is to examine these moral concerns about eating meat. As the title suggests, I'll be arguing vegetarians are mistaken in their conviction that meat-eating is morally wrong. It's OK to eat meat, even when it's produced in the objectionable ways that are common today. Moreover, it's possible to do these things while still being a person of integrity, principle, and public spirit—and while condemning the processes through which meat is brought to our restaurants, supermarkets, and dinner tables.

In case it needs to be said: I will *not* be arguing that eating meat automatically makes you a person of virtue, integrity, and public spirit. Most meat-eaters undoubtedly have a variety of grounds for re-examining their lives. (Don't we all?) I also won't claim it's inherently misguided to abstain from meat. If you're inclined to avoid it, you'll find no objections to that choice from me. As I'll discuss in greater depth below, eating meat is neither necessary nor sufficient for a life well lived. This book only claims that eating meat is morally OK and thus *compatible* with an ethical life—just like countless other permissible actions such as buying a house, working in retail, and wearing a sweater when it's cold outside.

Before launching in, let me make a brief note about terminology. Morally-motivated critics of meat-eating go by many names that reflect subtle differences in what they believe. For example, "vegetarians" commonly eat eggs and dairy products, but "vegans" do not. "Ostrovegans" eat bivalves like oysters and mussels on the premise that their nervous systems are too simple to make them conscious. "Freegans" don't buy animal products but will eat them if others have thrown them away.[2]

These camps disagree with one another about how we ought to eat, but they all share a common belief we must not eat meat "in the regular way." To eat meat "in the regular way," I take it, is to do so whenever one feels like it, without necessarily paying close attention to the details of how the meat was produced. A person who eats meat "in the regular way" will feel no hesitation ordering it at a restaurant, for example, if the relevant menu item sounds tasty. Likewise, a person who eats meat "in the regular way" will readily buy it at the grocery store to cook at home—and not just the "fancy" meat from the ultra-conscientious producers, but also the mainstream stuff filling most of the space on the shelves.

Since I'll be arguing it *is* OK to eat meat "in the regular way," the differences between the various anti-meat outlooks are inessential for our discussion. For the sake of simplicity, I'll use the word "vegetarian" as an umbrella term for my interlocutors. My position in what follows is simple: vegetarians in all their stripes are mistaken when they deny it's morally OK to eat meat.

IN SEARCH OF GOOD ARGUMENTS

As a sociological matter, it might appear my side of the debate has long held the upper hand. Despite the millions practicing vegetarianism worldwide, the vast majority of people continue to eat meat. Indeed, global meat consumption has been steadily on the rise.[3] Even most people who experiment with vegetarianism eventually go back to meat, many after just a few months. In the United States, for example, the Humane Research Council found in 2014 that 12.1% of Americans have been vegetarians at one point (including vegans), with only 1.9% currently practicing vegetarianism and 10.2% claiming to have done so in the past—a reversion rate of about 84%.[4]

Yet vegetarians can offer numerous explanations for these facts that have little to do with the ethical merits of meat-eating. As I've already said, many around the world are too poor to be choosy about food. Among those who can afford more discretion, some aren't aware of the moral objections to eating meat. Others are familiar with the objections but simply don't care. Many people are convinced it's OK to eat meat only because they embrace silly, easily refutable arguments. Some believe it's wrong but lack the willpower to follow through on this conviction. By appealing to explanations like these, vegetarians can plausibly argue that even though most people *in fact* eat meat, this doesn't prove meat-eaters have persuasive arguments to defend what they do.[5]

We can raise further doubts by considering some common arguments for why eating meat is OK. Many meat-eaters justify their actions by appealing to meat's deliciousness or its role in sustaining our health. Some fixate on the "naturalness" of meat-eating, while others point to religious texts as providing authoritative guidance on the subject. For better or worse, all of these arguments are unconvincing. Let's examine them in turn.

ENJOYABLE?

It would be no use denying the deliciousness of meat. In the eyes of some meat-eaters, this is enough to prove it's OK to eat it. But although this sort of consideration may explain why people *enjoy* eating meat, it's not very useful for showing the *moral acceptability* of doing so. We know from other areas of life that morality regularly condemns actions with the potential to produce pleasure. It would be nice to have others' belongings, for example, but that doesn't justify theft. It would be nice to have people do stuff for you, but that doesn't justify slavery. We find across many domains that pleasantness doesn't always equal moral permissibility. Meat's deliciousness doesn't prove, then, that it's morally OK to eat it.

One response might be that meat-eating isn't just pleasant: it's essential for happiness. The unique flavors and textures of meat might be so peerless among foods that a life without them would be stunted and flat.[6] If giving up meat would close off the possibility of true happiness, that would provide a stronger case for meat-eating than the mere observation that meat tastes good.[7]

There are two problems with this reply, however. First, it simply seems false that vegetarians cannot be happy. Many plant-based foods are delicious, and the world's culinary traditions offer countless opportunities for fulfilling meatless experiences.[8] Indeed, vegetarians who play their cards right can plausibly draw even more pleasure from their diets than many meat-eaters do. Insofar as they believe they're doing what's right, vegetarians also get a bonus of feeling good about themselves when they sit down for a meal.[9] Empirically speaking, psychological studies of the reported wellbeing of vegetarians and meat-eaters tend to find little meaningful difference between the two groups.[10]

However, a second problem with this line of argument is that even if eating meat *were* necessary for happiness, this could hardly vindicate doing it "in the regular way." The instances of meat-eating that significantly impact our lives are few and far between. When I order pork instead of tofu in my restaurant stir-fry, this choice has no important ramifications for the overall quality of my life. Nor does my happiness depend on whether I roll my homemade burrito with chicken or beans. Especially when one considers the many uninteresting and even disgusting meat dishes one encounters as an omnivore, it seems clear happiness would be possible while cutting the majority of meat from our diets. At most, appealing to meat's unique culinary importance could justify eating it only on special occasions—and plausibly not even then.

It's worth noting in this connection that many meat-eaters find it difficult to consider becoming vegetarian because this would mean giving up on things like Thanksgiving turkey (in the United States) or a special meal prepared by a family member. Vegetarians tend to believe these experiences are worth sacrificing to maintain a meat-free diet.[11] But even if giving up these specific food items were too much to ask, this would hardly undermine the case for giving up meat *at other times.* Thus, even if we accepted its dubious premise, this kind of argument would be a poor fit for defending meat-eating "in the regular way."

HEALTHY?

Another common argument for eating meat is that it's necessary for health. Meat is an important dietary source of protein and micronutrients like iron, vitamin A, and vitamin B12. In fact, vitamin B12—which, among other things, is essential for building red blood cells and DNA—is found in no commonly eaten foods besides animal products. On the basis of considerations like these, some people claim eating meat is required for health.[12]

Although no one would dispute the importance of staying healthy, this argument runs into the same two problems as the previous one. First, the argument's central claim appears false: medical professionals broadly agree it's possible to maintain a healthy diet while avoiding meat and other animal products.[13] Vegetarians need to ensure they eat certain foods to get the nutrients they need, but it's widely accepted this can be done. Even vitamin B12 turns out to be produced by particular algae, so vegetarians can obtain it easily from supplements that conform to their dietary principles.

Second, even if we did need meat to be healthy, this certainly wouldn't vindicate the vast majority of actual meat-eating. Especially in developed nations, most meat-eaters consume far more meat than is required for their health. In fact, *overconsumption* of meat is linked to major public health problems such as heart disease and obesity.[14] For the typical meat-eater, appealing to health thus cannot justify more than a small fraction of their consumption. Once again, we find that anyone hoping to defend meat-eating "in the regular way" will need a different kind of argument.

Notice a pattern that's beginning to emerge. When meat-eaters argue we have to eat meat to be happy, healthy, or whatever, the idea is that meat-eating is somehow *necessary*— without it, people can't flourish. All arguments of this form face the same two obstacles. On the one hand, it simply seems false that meat is necessary in any important sense. Whether or not one finds vegetarianism appealing, it goes too far to claim such a diet is incompatible with human welfare. But even if eating meat really were necessary, it's implausible this necessity would extend to eating meat "in the regular way." Maybe there are some cases in which we really do *have to* eat meat. But almost none of our actual meat-eating falls into this category.[15]

We shouldn't be surprised to find that arguments of the form "But I have to do it!" are unconvincing. Usually, when people resort to this type of argument, it's because they're doing something bad—and usually, they're lying. For those who hope to provide a satisfying defense of meat-eating, it's best to avoid arguments with this form. If eating meat is a morally dubious act that can only be justified by its necessity, the debate has already been lost.

NATURAL?

Some defenses of eating meat avoid appeals to necessity. These arguments claim meat-eating isn't objectionable in the first place, so it's OK even when we don't strictly *have to* do it. This is a more promising strategy, but even many arguments of this type are unconvincing.

One example is the claim that eating meat is OK because it's "natural."[16] This line of reasoning may be supported in a variety of ways. For instance, it can be argued that humans have been eating meat for our whole history as a species. Certain features of our biology—for example, our canine teeth—seem especially suited to this task. Moreover, meat-eating is not a distinctively human activity: primates have been doing it since long before humans evolved, and many other animals eat meat as well. Not only is meat-eating a normal feature of animal life on earth, but it plays an essential role in the functioning of natural ecosystems. Meat-eating is thus a thoroughly natural phenomenon: it's natural for humans, and it's natural more broadly as well.

We should be careful not to interpret this argument as just another appeal to necessity. The claim is not that if we stopped eating meat, it would invite ecological collapse, species extinctions, or some other environmental calamity.[17] (If that were the argument, it would run into the same problems as above. Ecological functioning doesn't typically require humans to eat meat. But even if it did, this wouldn't justify the farming practices that produce most of our actual meat—not least because these practices often harm the environment.) The sort of argument I have in mind here is more fundamental. It holds that eating meat is natural, and there can be no reasonable objection to activities that are natural in this way.

One problem with this kind of argument is that many "natural" things should be avoided or stopped.[18] For example, it's "natural" for people to murder one another in a struggle for power and resources: humans have been doing this for as long as they've existed,[19] and other animals do it as well. Throughout history, people skeptical of morality have reminded us that the natural order allows the strong to do as they wish, whether that involves theft, slavery, murder, etc.[20] Yet, observations like these hardly reflect what's morally justifiable. If anything, morality is a system for reorienting behavior away from these sorts of "natural" behaviors toward equity and justice.

Making matters worse, meat-eating looks on its surface like many of the "natural" practices we regard as immoral. Like theft, slavery, and murder, meat-eating appears to impose massive costs on helpless individuals (most obviously animals, but also people impacted negatively by meat production) in the name of self-interest. If morality teaches us anything about "nature," it's that we should regard behaviors bearing these characteristics with extreme suspicion.

For reasons like these, appeals to the "naturalness" of meat-eating yield an unconvincing defense. Far from proving it's OK to eat meat, such arguments virtually beg vegetarians to draw an analogy between meat-eating and other notorious forms of immorality. The "naturalness" of meat-eating may provide a *factual* explanation for why it's so common (just as it helps explain the existence of theft, slavery, and murder). But it hardly gives us an ethical argument for continuing to do it.

ENDORSED BY GOD?

Another defense of eating meat draws support from religious texts such as the Holy Bible. Many regard these texts as authoritative guides to morality, and it's possible to find several passages that seem clearly supportive of meat-eating. For example, in the book of Genesis, God explicitly tells Noah, "Every moving thing that lives shall be food for you."[21] For people of faith, such passages may seem to vindicate meat-eating regardless of what arguments vegetarians can muster.

This isn't a book about religion, and most of what follows will not focus on religious arguments. However, it would be a mistake to ignore the topic of religion entirely. Since some might see Biblical support for meat-eating as eliminating the need for further defense of the practice, it will help motivate this book to explain why things aren't as simple as this.

One difficulty with scriptural justifications of meat-eating is that even within religious texts themselves, it's not always clear a single viewpoint is being articulated about the propriety of eating meat. For example, although God grants Noah the right to eat meat, this departs from the standard He had set up to that point. When God first created humans, He assigned them *dominion* over the other animals, but this *did not* include a right to eat meat. (God said, "See, I have given you every plant yielding seed that is upon the face of all the earth, and every tree with seed in its fruit; you shall have them for food."[22]) God's instructions to Noah represented a change in the rules:

referring back to His original arrangement with Adam, God said to Noah, "Just as I gave you the green plants, I give you everything."[23]

By the time we get to Leviticus, it once again seems God has altered his guidance about what can and can't be eaten. Whereas Noah was told he could eat *every* moving thing that lives, Leviticus forbids eating numerous creatures, including camels, hyraxes, rabbits, pigs, and many others.[24] As we continue forward to Isaiah's prophecies, we find indication that killing animals may be headed out of fashion altogether. Isaiah envisions a world in which even nonhuman predators have abandoned their bloodthirsty ways[25] and "Whoever slaughters an ox is like one who kills a human being ...."[26]

These repeated shifts in the Bible's guidance and tone make it hard to appeal to individual passages to vindicate meat-eating once and for all. Even if we unreservedly accept the Bible's moral authority, we can see plainly from its text that eating meat has been supported in certain contexts and not others. It's not open-and-shut that just because we can find support for meat-eating in the Bible, it must be OK. There's always the possibility it *was* OK for people in a particular time or place but should nevertheless be avoided today.

This concern is reinforced by the Bible's apparent endorsement of several other practices we now regard as clearly unacceptable. For example, several Biblical passages appear to endorse slavery and even provide guidance for how slaves should be acquired and managed.[27] One startling passage in Exodus delineates the rule that "When a slaveowner strikes a male or female slave with a rod and the slave dies immediately, the owner shall be punished. But if the slave survives a day or two, there is no punishment; for the slave is the owner's property."[28] The Bible also mandates a penalty of death for wide-ranging offenses we now regard as either insufficient grounds for such extreme retribution (such as cursing one's parents or committing adultery)[29] or inappropriate bases for any retribution whatsoever (such as engaging in gay sex).[30]

These scriptural elements present an interpretive challenge. How can believers simultaneously hold the moral authority of sacred texts beyond doubt without thereby accepting the legitimacy of rules and practices like these? Numerous strategies exist for resolving this puzzle. For example, some have claimed that when Biblical texts appear to endorse practices that are wrong for us to engage in, we must understand the relevant passages as restricted to their particular contexts and not applicable outside them.[31] Others insist scripture is not always meant to be taken literally, and certain passages require subtle allegorical or holistic interpretations to be properly understood.[32] Many other reconciliatory strategies also exist, but all help highlight the fact that conscientious believers must find *some* strategy to explain why apparent scriptural endorsements of objectionable behaviors don't license those behaviors for us.

Once we begin down this road, however, it seems clear there will be trouble in appealing to scripture to defend meat-eating. Whatever strategy we deploy to explain why we ought to abstain from things like owning slaves or killing those who curse their parents—despite apparent Biblical support for these practices—vegetarians can sensibly ask why we don't apply this strategy to think about meat-eating as well. Why not interpret favorable discussions of meat-eating as affixed to a particular context, as allegory, or as requiring interpretation through the lens of broader Biblical values? Why would pointing to scriptural passages justify meat-eating in the face of vegetarians' substantive objections but *not* justify other morally dubious practices?

For Christians, matters are complicated still further by the idea that what ultimately counts for ethical purposes is not compliance with specific rules of conduct but rather one's quality of will and faith in God. In the Gospel of Mark, Jesus asks,

> Do you not see that whatever goes into a person from the outside cannot defile, since it enters, not the heart but the stomach, and goes out into the sewer? ... It is what comes out of a person that defiles. For it is from within, from the human heart, that evil intentions come ....[33]

In his first letter to the Corinthians, Paul echoes this idea, adding that "whatever you eat or drink or whatever you do, do it all for the glory of God."[34] Through the lens of statements like these, it seems the important question is not whether eating meat is *intrinsically* acceptable, but rather whether doing it is consistent with moral uprightness in a more general sense. Perhaps scripture could be cited to insist some vegetarians err in focusing on *the meat itself* instead of the meat-eater's character. But plainly, vegetarians believe a person of good character would avoid eating meat, and refuting this claim requires carefully rebutting their arguments. Here once again, we may cite Paul: "'I have the right to do anything,' you say—but not everything is beneficial. 'I have the right to do anything,' you say—but not everything is constructive."[35]

None of this is to say scripture provides a knock-down case for vegetarianism.[36] The point is simply that, as with so many controversial issues, pointing to sacred texts is unlikely to provide a decisive resolution to our disagreements. Although it might be nice to simply open a book and receive divine revelation about how to live, there's no substitute in this context for examining the merits of competing viewpoints.

THE OTHER SIDE OF THE COIN

We have now considered a number of unconvincing arguments for why it's OK to eat meat. At their best, these arguments left major unresolved questions; at their worst, they offered little more than smokescreens. If meat-eaters hope to defend their choices against vegetarian critiques, they need different and better arguments.

Lest meat-eaters feel picked on, I hasten to note vegetarians have not been immune to bad arguments either—far from it. To cite just one example, in a mirror image of a pro-meat argument considered earlier, some vegetarians insist we must give up meat to protect our health.[37] Again, the starting premise seems false: virtually all medical professionals agree it's possible to be healthy while eating (some) meat.[38] But even if it were true, it still wouldn't imply meat-eating is wrong. Plenty of things are bad for our health but OK to do—especially in moderation. If meat were really unhealthy, then *at most*, this would show it's imprudent to consume too much of it, just as it's imprudent to consume too much candy, alcohol, or caffeine.[39]

The debate over meat-eating is rife with arguments so bad they can be refuted in just a few paragraphs. Yet, my purpose in this book is not to catalog poorly conceived arguments. Rather, my goal is to examine the strongest arguments on each side in order to ultimately show it's OK to eat meat. Instead of focusing on the silly things people say, let's turn to the task of debating the best arguments for vegetarianism and developing a convincing case for why, despite all vegetarians have said, it's OK to eat meat after all.

PLAN FOR THE BOOK

Ethical vegetarians have a seemingly straightforward position: eating meat is wrong. However, things get complicated when we try to clarify the explanation for *why* it's wrong. Vegetarians offer many different reasons. Let's consider a few. Mainstream "factory farming" cruelly mistreats animals, some say, and we shouldn't support this practice. Animals' moral significance is no different from our own, so eating them is just as disrespectful as eating one another—or at least humans with similar capacities to animals, such as those with severe cognitive limitations. Animals are our fellow creatures, and properly appreciating them as such rules out viewing them as food. Corporate meat producers grossly mistreat their employees, and we should show solidarity with workers by boycotting their companies' products. Animal agriculture produces massive environmental impacts, and giving up meat would reduce our ecological footprints. The way we raise animals increases the risk of new pandemics, and public safety demands we mitigate these risks. If everyone stopped eating meat, the world would be a better place. People ought to avoid eating meat in order to stand up to misbehaving meat companies and distance themselves from the industry's wrongdoing. It's wrong to take pleasure from consuming something connected to so many serious problems. And on and on and on...

Some vegetarians consider it a good thing for their cause that there are so many anti-meat arguments.[40] It seems to suggest their position is almost certainly correct and would not be undermined if one or two arguments turned out to be misguided. On the other hand, the vast number of vegetarian arguments makes things difficult for someone aiming to challenge the view. For any attack on one particular argument for vegetarianism, it will always be possible for the vegetarian to respond, "OK, but what about ...?" To have a hope of making progress in this book, it won't do to take on every argument at once. Instead, we'll need to slow down and consider the individual arguments in turn.[41]

We can simplify our task by distinguishing between two broad families of vegetarian ethical arguments: the "wrong in practice" arguments and the "wrong in principle" arguments. "Wrong in practice" arguments link the wrongness of eating meat to how nearly all of it is produced today. These arguments claim we ought to be vegetarians because of meat industry practices that are cruel, exploitative, environmentally destructive, and unsafe. Such arguments have been influential for many vegetarians, but they're not the only ones that guide the movement. "Wrong in principle" arguments hold we ought not to eat meat *regardless of how it's produced*.[42] These arguments insist meat-eating implies disrespect or lack of appreciation for other animals, with the implication that it would still be wrong to eat meat even if all animals were raised humanely, equitably, sustainably, and safely.

The difference between these two families of argument is important because some meat-eaters share vegetarians' concerns about "factory-farmed" meat but, rather than avoiding meat altogether, try to *transform* it into something more ethically sensitive and engaged. These so-called "conscientious omnivores" embody an important alternative to the standard vegetarian position that it's wrong to eat meat. In their view, it's wrong to eat *certain* meat—indeed, *most* meat, given how the modern meat industry operates—but there are nevertheless cases where it's OK to eat meat because of the careful practices producers adopt.[43]

Because of these "conscientious omnivores," vegetarians can't fully defend the claim that it's wrong to eat meat by simply pointing to the meat industry's problems. Conscientious omnivores advance the same concerns while still maintaining it's sometimes OK to eat meat. To completely vindicate their position, vegetarians need to show there's something about eating meat *as such* that makes it impossible to do while being truly conscientious. This is where "wrong in principle" arguments come in, working to show that even if animals were raised unimpeachably, it would still be immoral to eat them.

Chapter 2 examines a selection of these "wrong in principle" arguments and shows why they fail, arguing vegetarians are mistaken to claim it's *inherently* wrong to eat meat. If all meat were produced humanely, equitably, sustainably, and safely, then it's highly plausible that eating it would be morally OK. This conclusion is quite limited, however, in what it can show. In a world where the vast majority of meat production is *not* humane, equitable, sustainable, and safe, the *possibility* of ethical meat production can't vindicate much actual meateating. To justify eating meat "in the regular way," the meat industry's true practices need to be confronted. What needs to be shown is how it could be OK to eat meat even when it results from practices that raise serious concerns about animals, workers, the environment, and public health. This much more difficult task constitutes the primary focus of this book.

Chapter 3 begins this discussion by surveying the meat industry's typical practices and exploring what standards are appropriate for evaluating its conduct. I focus special attention on how chickens, pigs, and cows are raised and slaughtered, given that these examples illustrate the main problems that preoccupy vegetarians and are seen by many as especially clear instances of wrongdoing. I show that, although there's room for disagreement about the best standards for evaluating the meat industry's conduct, there's strong reason to think the industry fails to satisfy even the most modest acceptable standards—particularly in its treatment of animals.

The analysis of Chapter 3 shows there's something wrong with how the meat industry conducts its business. But further exploration is needed to establish what this means for *consumers*. As David DeGrazia puts the point in his own defense of vegetarianism

> Factory farming is morally indefensible. What follows for individuals' responsibilities? Nothing follows straightforwardly, so we will need arguments to cross the bridge from institutional wrong to individual obligation.[44]

Chapters 4–6 examine a variety of vegetarian pathways for trying to establish that the wr0ongness of the meat industry's actions means each of us is obligated to abstain from meat. Chapter 4 considers arguments that focus on the *impacts* of eating or avoiding meat—whether at the individual level or the level of the broader vegetarian movement. Chapter 5 explores arguments that employ the test of universalization to ask: what if people generally behaved the way meat-eaters (or vegetarians) do? Chapter 6 discusses arguments regarding how we position ourselves in relationship to the meat industry's problems—how we express our convictions, implicate ourselves in its conduct, and engage emotionally with its products.

The thesis that emerges from these chapters is that vegetarianism offers a valuable *option* for responding to an important set of problems, but it's only one such option and hence not one we're specifically obligated to choose. I argue that, in a world full of urgent problems and undesirable social patterns, each of us has a duty to try to help make the world a morally better place. But given the many ways in which we can satisfy that duty, vegetarianism fails to stand out as a single form of activism each of us is morally required to take up.

Ultimately, this book is meant not simply as a defense of meat-eating but also as a more general call to action. Most of us—meat-eaters and vegetarians alike—realize our world is full of serious problems. Most of us also realize we're doing less about these problems than we should. Although I deny we have a specific duty to respond to the meat industry's problems by giving up meat, vegetarians' mistake doesn't come from being totally off base. The problem with the position taken by ethical vegetarians is that it narrowly interprets a moral imperative that's actually much broader. We don't have a specific duty to become vegetarians, but we *do* have a duty to help make the world a better place. The claim I'll defend is that it's up to us to decide how.

Two

Almost no one—including meat-eaters—thinks it's OK to kill and eat other people. What's more, this prohibition on people-eating seems to apply even to delicate forms of cannibalism. To illustrate, imagine I raise some children with great care, treating all the children's caretakers with respect and meticulously avoiding ecological impacts and public health risks. These measures notwithstanding, if I painlessly killed the children in their sleep and ate their flesh, I'd be a moral monster. The immorality of treating other humans as foodstuffs doesn't depend on the specific ways we might raise and kill them. Even the most careful approach to farming humans would still be morally unacceptable.

Vegetarians often make arguments that portray meat-eating in a similar light. According to these arguments, the wrongness of eating meat isn't *solely* a product of the practices we use to raise and slaughter animals (though vegetarians object to these as well). Even if we replaced existing practices with humane, equitable, sustainable, and safe alternatives, many vegetarians would still regard meat-eating as immoral. Tom Regan, for example, argues the basic problem with eating meat is that it fails to show respect for animals as more than mere means to our dietary ends. To him and others with similar views, thorough reforms to our farming operations

DOI: 10.4324/9781003221944-2

"would not alter the basic injustice of the practice; it would only eliminate the further wrong of harming these individuals in this way. It would make the implementation of the practice *less* wrong, but it would not remove the fundamental injustice endemic to the practice."[1] As long as meat-eaters continue viewing animals as potential menu items rather than individuals deserving of respect, vegetarians like Regan insist they'll remain morally in the wrong. And this will be true no matter how painstakingly we transform farming to avoid animal cruelty, worker mistreatment, environmental degradation, or public health risks.

The view that eating meat is wrong *in principle* will be the subject of this chapter. From the start, I should emphasize that even if we reject this outlook and declare it's *possible* to be a "conscientious omnivore," there may still be powerful reasons to worry about eating meat in reality, given the problematic ways in which it's *actually* produced.[2] Indeed, given that this book devotes only one chapter to "wrong in principle" arguments—and four to the view that meat-eating is wrong because of the practical realities of its production—this should signal that the arguments of this chapter represent only one step toward showing it's OK to eat meat. However, this step is essential because if raising and killing animals for food were *inherently* immoral, it would be unnecessary to get bogged down in the meat industry's real-world problems. If even the most ethically sensitive animal farming would still be unacceptable, issues of "factory farming" and the like would be beside the point. Since I believe these practical matters are actually at the heart of the issue, let's turn to the task of making plausible the view that eating meat *could be* OK—at least in principle, if it were produced conscientiously—in order to clear the way for debating whether it's OK in the world we actually inhabit.

Some of the best-known arguments for the "wrong in principle" view revolve around the idea that—at least when it comes to whether something can legitimately be raised and killed for food—there's no sharp moral difference between what humans and animals are due. Insofar as it's categorically wrong to kill and eat humans, the argument goes, the same must be true about animals.

If you've spent time around vegetarians, you've likely heard some version of this claim. Yet, the position demands clarification since it tends to strike meat-eaters as bizarre if not obviously misguided. On the face of things, there appear to be many differences between humans and animals that seem relevant to why eating humans might be "wrong in principle" while eating animals might not be. For example, human lives contain *meaning* in ways animal lives do not. A human can reflect on their life as a whole and pursue projects that fit together in an integrated way; they can self-consciously cultivate a personality, an identity, and a character; and they can develop rich relationships with others based on compatible interests, values, and aspirations. Humans can also *cooperate* with others in ways animals cannot. They can treat others with respect and demand others reciprocate; they can restrain their actions to honor moral reasons and social rules; and they can sacrifice their self-interest in the name of justice, beneficence, and commitment to a higher cause. Considering characteristics like these, there may seem to be little mystery why we cannot legitimately regard humans as foodstuffs. Likewise, there may seem to be little mystery why we *can* regard animals that way, given that they lack these characteristics that underpin the respect humans are due.

However, vegetarian authors have highlighted an important problem with this way of thinking. The problem comes from the fact that, even among humans, there are individuals who lack the characteristics listed above. Some humans are born with cognitive disabilities so severe their lives will never contain substantially more meaning than the lives of animals we eat. Some humans will never fully participate in our systems of ethical cooperation. Yet, we don't generally think these humans deserve dramatically less care and respect than their more cognitively sophisticated relatives, and we certainly don't think it's OK to raise and kill them for food.[3]

If this is true, it suggests our attitudes of care and respect can't be based *solely* on characteristics like one's capacity for meaningfully organizing one's life or for moral cooperation, for this would exclude humans who lack such characteristics. Any universal human trait that could justify our attitudes toward the severely cognitively disabled would seemingly need to be "some lowest common denominator, pitched so low no human lacks them."[4] Yet vegetarians rightly observe that any such "lowest common denominator" characteristics (e.g., the capacity for pleasure and pain, or the ability to consciously experience one's life) will inevitably be possessed by other animals as well. So, whatever we think these characteristics demand when we find them in humans, the vegetarians' point is that we'll have precisely the same reason to think they're morally significant when we find them in other animals.

It may be surprising to learn that the philosopher most famous for highlighting the overlap between the characteristics of animals and severely cognitively disabled humans—Peter Singer—actually did not interpret the comparison as showing it's "wrong in principle" to eat meat. In his classic book, *Animal Liberation*, Singer explicitly considers the possibility of eating "free-range animals … who have a pleasant existence in a social group suited to their behavioral needs, and are then killed quickly and without pain." He writes,

> I can respect conscientious people who take care to eat only meat that comes from such animals—but I suspect that unless they live on a farm where they can look after their own animals, they will, in practice, be very nearly vegetarian anyway.[5]

To Singer, it's not wrong in principle to eat meat: the true case for vegetarianism revolves around how meat is produced in practice.

Predictably, however, other vegetarians—not to mention disability activists[6]—have found this aspect of Singer's position alarming. If we take seriously Singer's analogy between animals and severely cognitively disabled humans, his endorsement of "conscientious" forms of animal agriculture would seem to imply that farming humans could be acceptable as well—at least in principle—if it were done with sufficient sensitivity and care.[7] To avoid this conclusion, a number of vegetarians have repurposed Singer's analogy in support of the claim that if a being exhibits key "lowest common denominator" characteristics which animals share with severely cognitively disabled humans, then it also bears a moral entitlement against being raised and killed for food— regardless of how it's treated along the way—and must receive the full consideration we consider appropriate for our cognitively disabled relatives.[8]

Some meat-eaters may be tempted to reject as absurd any outlook according to which animals deserve moral consideration on a par with human beings. One might ask, for example,

"If animals are our equals, does that mean they should get the right to vote?" However, this type of objection rests on a misunderstanding. To demand equal *care and respect* is not the same as demanding equal *treatment*. Since voting requires the sophisticated cognitive faculties we discussed earlier, the right to vote applies only to individuals who have those faculties. So, it's true animals can't have this right, but it's also true severely cognitively disabled humans can't have it. Indeed, we don't ascribe a right to vote even to children we expect to grow into brilliant, caring, public-spirited adults. The key point is that even though children (and severely cognitively disabled adults) lack characteristics that underpin *certain* rights and privileges, we nevertheless regard them as fully deserving of care and respect in the ways that are relevant to them.

Proponents of the "wrong in principle" perspective believe we should extend this same standard to animals. In their view, animals should be respected and cared for in ways that are relevant to them. This would not mean doing things like empowering them to vote (which would be ridiculous) but rather honoring their interests and not viewing them as commodities to be raised and killed for our culinary enjoyment.[9]

DEBUNKING RESPECT?

Tying moral status to "lowest common denominator" characteristics yields a seemingly intuitive explanation for why even humans with severe cognitive disabilities deserve consideration just like the rest of us.[10] Given vegetarians' convictions about the moral status of animals, it's also a happy outcome in their eyes that such an outlook implies we have stringent obligations toward animals. Yet this approach generates an important philosophical puzzle. In the previous section, when we discussed characteristics commonly thought to distinguish humans from animals, I said many people think humans deserve respect *because* of their capacities to live meaningful, integrated lives and participate in systems of moral cooperation. According to such perspectives, animals don't deserve the same level of respect as humans *because they lack* these advanced characteristics. The underlying supposition is that our distinguishing human capacities help make sense of the respect we owe one another.

Vegetarians struck by the overlap between animals' capabilities and those of severely cognitively disabled humans deny these characteristics put a being on a different moral plane from others who lack them. In their view, grounding elevated moral status on humans' sophisticated cognitive abilities is just as misguided as saying a person merits extra moral consideration for being able to play the cello or walk a tightrope. Yet, suppose we grant that whether a being can live a meaningful life or cooperate morally makes no difference to its moral status. Why would the upshot be that *animals* deserve the level of consideration we currently show *humans* (including those with severe cognitive disabilities)? Why wouldn't it be that *humans* deserve no more consideration than we currently show *animals*?

To frame the issue more clearly, suppose Alice (a typical meat-eater) starts with a moral outlook that recognizes two levels of moral status—a level demanding "compassion," which she applies to animals, and a higher level demanding "respect," which she applies to humans. The "compassionate" level of consideration, as Alice conceives it, is founded on characteristics possessed by all animals, including humans. These creatures can suffer, experience their lives, and so on. Hence, as she sees it, they are worthy of being treated *humanely* and not simply as objects to be used however we please. This compassionate level of consideration might stand in tension with inhumane forms of animal farming (as we'll discuss in greater depth in Chapter 3). But Alice nevertheless believes it's *possible* to farm and kill a being for food while showing it adequate compassion (say, by providing it a pleasant life full of species-appropriate experiences and ensuring its death comes painlessly and without fear).

If human beings deserved nothing more than compassion, Alice might see nothing wrong with treating them the way "conscientious omnivores" propose to treat livestock. But of course, Alice doesn't accept this: she believes humans deserve not just compassion but *respect*. This higher level of consideration—which Alice intuitively takes to be grounded in distinctively human characteristics like the capacities to live a meaningful life and cooperate morally—demands more than just humane treatment. In Alice's view, properly respecting someone rules out raising and killing them for food as a matter of principle.

Now suppose Alice reads this chapter and becomes convinced that having these distinctively human characteristics makes no difference to what level of consideration a being is due. The consideration due to an individual with such characteristics is no different from that due to one who lacks them, and in fact, there's nothing about the most cognitively sophisticated humans that places them on a different plane of consideration from an animal like a chicken, pig, or cow. Given that Alice had construed her attitudes of respect *as a response to* humans' distinctive cognitive characteristics, wouldn't the sensible upshot of rejecting these characteristics' salience be to assign all animals—human and otherwise—the "compassionate" level of consideration? Why shouldn't Alice discard the "respectful" level of consideration as an error based on assumptions she now sees as false?

An analogy may help reinforce this point. Historically, it was believed certain individuals qualified for special moral consideration on the basis of their "royal blood." These royals were regarded as deserving special deference from commoners (known as "fealty"). Likewise, they were seen as having an inborn right to rule over non-royals. Thankfully, people today have come to reject the idea there is any such moral plane as "royalty" that's elevated over the rest of us. Yet, the upshot of rejecting this idea was not that *everyone* should be regarded as a king or queen. Rather, it was that *no one* merits the status of royals. Suppose we likewise come to believe that moral distinctions grounded in our capacities to live meaningful lives and cooperate morally are just as baseless as those which were once grounded in "royal blood." In this case, why wouldn't the upshot be that we should abandon those distinctions as we did with the idea of "royalty?" Why shouldn't we view our notion of "respect" as unfounded and conclude nobody deserves a level of consideration beyond what's demanded by "compassion"?

THE NEED FOR AN EXPLANATION

The most vocal proponents of "wrong in principle" arguments devote little attention to whether the entire idea of respect could be misguided. In keeping with most of our intuitions, they take for granted that respect is warranted *among human beings*. Their question is just whether we should extend the same sort of respect to animals. However, given their attacks on our traditional understandings of respect, it's debatable whether they're entitled to this complacency. The unquestioning attitude toward respect seems especially problematic when we examine the idea more closely and confront some very real mysteries about why it's justified.

Consider that if I steal something that's yours, I commit a moral offense against you—I treat you unjustly and thus disrespect you. Notice that this is true even if the thing I take has relatively little value to you and much greater value to me. For example, imagine I'm a painter who would be deprived of the ability to paint without access to your watercolor set. Imagine you're a wealthy dilettante who's bought some watercolors, used them a while, and set them aside to pursue other hobbies. If I steal your watercolors when you're not looking, I might gain far more than you lose—in fact, you might not notice anything missing for some time. Still, most of us would say I'm not permitted to steal your watercolors just because I value them more than you do. To take them without your permission would be unjust and disrespectful.

Observe, however, that this is not because we generally consider it disrespectful to set back others' interests when pursuing our goals. If you are a shopkeeper and I open a competing business down the street, I may lure away your customers and even bankrupt your store. This might be a major tragedy to you—one I caused through my actions, perhaps knowingly. Still, you couldn't claim I had acted *disrespectfully* by starting a business next to yours. I have a right to outcompete you in the marketplace, even if that spells disaster for your livelihood.

These judgments differ importantly from those that might flow from the ideal of compassion. If you're a wealthy dilettante who learns a poor artist will be unable to paint without your watercolors, compassion might properly impel you to give up your paint set. Likewise, a prospective business owner might be pushed by compassion to consider a different place to open a store upon learning a particular location would threaten another company. To say these are not matters of *respect* is not to say they're unimportant. It's simply to say that respect and compassion are different things that operate in fundamentally different ways.

The examples above help us see that respect is a strange thing that doesn't boil down simply to concern for others. Respect imposes certain constraints on what we can and can't do to one another, and it empowers us to make demands of others which they are duty-bound to honor. These constraints and demands don't line up straightforwardly with the strengths of the interests they are seemingly there to protect. Sometimes we have strong obligations to honor weak interests, and sometimes we have no obligation (of respect, as opposed to compassion) to honor strong ones.

This puzzling nature of respect seems to cry out for explanation. But the trouble for those who would seek to defend "in principle" objections to meat-eating is that, at least historically, moral theorists' efforts to make sense of respect have typically revolved around the distinctive human characteristics we discussed at the beginning of this chapter. Different moral theorists have emphasized different traits, and some have viewed certain traits as central that others have considered irrelevant. But it's nevertheless possible to see broad agreement on something like the following. Unlike other animals, humans live together in political societies governed by systems of rules. These rules create protected spheres in which people can plan and carry out projects that give their lives meaning without fearing others will harm or exploit them. These rules force people to sacrifice certain objectives that would come at others' expense. But they also provide valuable protection and the opportunity to organize one's life according to one's values and aspirations. By participating faithfully in these schemes, we express our commitment to our shared prosperity and affirm our common dignity as free and equal persons, enabling us all to flourish in distinctly human ways.[11]

Readers with academic backgrounds in philosophy will undoubtedly feel the urge to quibble with some of the details of this vague reconstruction. For our purposes, however, let's set these scholarly matters aside and consider how this general line of reasoning explains why it makes sense to affirm attitudes of respect that don't simply boil down to compassion. In the argument above, respect is cast as an integral component of a scheme of cooperation that underpins crucial human values, and it's seen to operate through systems of general rules and practices rather than simply on the basis of what's at stake in each particular situation. By focusing on the distinctive ways humans live, interact, and prosper, we can explain important aspects of our moral lives that might otherwise seem mysterious.

By insisting that none of humanity's distinctive characteristics have any bearing on the type of consideration humans are due, vegetarian writers make it mysterious why anyone merits respect instead of only compassion. Think back to the cases of the watercolors and the new business. We can perhaps make sense of why there are principled rules against stealing from people but not against outcompeting them in the marketplace when we consider the distinctive ways humans organize and carry out their lives in cooperative societies. But if we focus exclusively on our "lowest common denominator" characteristics—those we share with severely cognitively disabled humans, as well as nonhuman animals—the peculiar contours of respect seem puzzling once again. Like with the unfounded idea of "royalty," rejecting the foundations of respect raises serious questions about whether this idea is justified.

This difficulty for the proponents of lowest common denominator arguments arises because of the *explanatory relationship* between traditional ideas about respect and the distinctively human characteristics in which those ideas have been grounded. Defenders of the "lowest common denominator" approach have proceeded as if they can simply trade out the classic foundations for those of their choosing, replacing characteristics like our capacities for cooperating morally or for living meaningful lives with "lowest common denominator" alternatives. But things aren't so simple. Those original foundations were doing important work, helping explain *why* we ought to respect one another instead of merely showing each other compassion. With the alternative foundations these writers propose, the special forms of deference "respect" commands us to show one another begin to look unmotivated and bizarre.

Of course, nothing I've said proves respect *is* justified. Perhaps, like "royalty," the idea of "respect" belongs in the dustbin of history. But if one wants to make the case animals and humans *both* deserve respect (as proponents of the "wrong in principle" view have sought to do), then it behooves one to have some explanation for why respect is warranted at all. If principled vegetarian writers wish to deny these attitudes have anything to do with distinctively human characteristics (in contrast with what moral theorists have traditionally argued), then they owe us some alternative explanation—one that has not been forthcoming thus far. Without some such explanation, the straightforward upshot of their views would not be that animals deserve respect alongside humans. Rather, it would be that "respect" is similar to "royalty" in looking like a misguided idea based on erroneous beliefs about what matters for morality.

THE CHARGE OF DISCRIMINATION

For the sake of discussion, suppose we say—contrary to proponents of the lowest common denominator approach—that it *does* make a difference to a being's moral status whether it has characteristics like the capacities to live a meaningful life and cooperate morally. If we accept this, we can begin to explain why the respect most of us take for granted makes sense among cognitively sophisticated human beings. But we must again confront Peter Singer's challenging observation from the beginning of this chapter. How can we justify the way we act toward humans who *lack* these distinguishing traits? As I've said, some humans are born with cognitive disabilities so severe they will never develop the characteristics commonly thought to set people apart from other animals. Does this mean severely cognitively disabled humans lack the same moral status as the rest of us? Could we farm and eat these humans "compassionately" without doing anything wrong?

One tempting response is to say that even if *a particular human* lacks the traits which underlie humans' moral importance more generally, the fact they're still *human* means they deserve the same consideration as other humans.[12] Yet, there's an obvious rebuttal to this line of reasoning. In virtue of what does membership in the species *Homo sapiens* entitle a being to this special treatment? Is it just that these humans look like us? Is it that we're related? Can we really maintain that appeals to characteristics like appearance and family relationships (which hardly seem relevant in themselves to a being's moral status) are anything more than smokescreens for discrimination—what we might call "speciesism" in line with other unjust attitudes like racism and sexism?[13]

This is the charge numerous vegetarian authors have pressed against those who refuse equal status to nonhuman animals. Whatever moral consideration we think animals are due, they claim we must show the same level of consideration to all beings with similar traits along the dimensions that matter. If we think it's OK to farm and eat animals, we must be consistent and say it's also OK to farm and eat other relevantly similar beings—including severely cognitively disabled humans. Likewise, if we think it's wrong to farm and eat the humans, it must also be wrong to farm and eat animals. Whatever we decide, the claim is the answer must be consistent. And since no one expects us to give up on the idea that farming and eating humans is wrong, the salient alternative is to extend that view to apply to the animals we currently treat as foodstuffs.

How can meat-eaters respond to this argument? The first step is to clarify what they have in mind when they affirm it's wrong to eat humans with severe cognitive disabilities. To help achieve this clarity, let's consider an imaginary scenario. Sometime in the future, an incurable virus emerges that attacks humans' brains, permanently reducing their intelligence to that of a cow. The disease infects every human on Earth, so eventually, there are no more humans with the distinguishing characteristics we've been examining: no one is capable of living an especially meaningful life or participating in advanced schemes of moral cooperation. Humans don't disappear, however; they simply inhabit Earth's ecosystems like any other species of animal. Over time, the traces of human civilization are erased from the planet. One day, the Earth is discovered by intelligent space aliens. To provide delicious food for themselves, the alien settlers begin farming animals—including humans. (For the sake of discussion, suppose they do this in line with the most demanding "conscientious omnivore" standards.) The aliens, unaware of the history of life on Earth, place no more significance on the humans than on the other animals they farm. Hence, they raise and kill many humans for food, showing them no more or less consideration than "conscientious omnivores" would have us show animals.

The critics of "speciesism" would seem correct to say that, whatever we consider appropriate when it comes to our treatment of animals, we'd better apply that same standard when evaluating the aliens' treatment of the severely cognitively limited humans. If we think it's OK to farm and eat cows—say, provided it's done humanely, equitably, sustainably, and safely—then consistency would seem to demand saying the aliens behave permissibly as well. If we don't accept this, then the anti-speciesists would be right to wonder why this is so. The creatures being treated as livestock in the story seem analogous in terms of their morally relevant characteristics to animals meat-eaters currently regard as livestock. It's not clear why the mere fact they're *Homines sapientes* should entitle them to a different standard of consideration.

For this point to serve as vindication for vegetarianism, however, it would need to be the case that meat-eaters can't sensibly accept the aliens behave permissibly in the story. But is this conclusion unacceptable? Speaking for myself as a meat-eater, I feel no inclination to resist it. As long as we grant that the humans in the story are reduced irreversibly to the cognitive level of cows, it seems appropriate to infer that what they deserve from space aliens is essentially the same as what cows deserve from us. Insofar as one believes this level of deservingness is compatible with being raised and killed for food when this is done humanely, equitably, sustainably, and safely, it seems unproblematic to say that what the aliens do in the story is OK.

However, a further and more troubling question is whether, by granting it's OK for *space aliens* to eat severely cognitively limited humans in the story, we thereby commit ourselves to say that it's also OK for *us* to treat our disabled relatives like foodstuffs. Some vegetarian authors have written as if this sort of symmetrical thinking follows straightforwardly, and only "speciesism" could lead us to deny it.[14] But presumably, meat-eaters will resist this further conclusion. Several considerations might be marshaled in defense of drawing a distinction between the two cases. For example, in the real world, a severely cognitively limited human is not a being we encounter simply by chance. Such an individual is someone's child and often also someone's sibling, cousin, or neighbor. Severely cognitively disabled humans are loved and honored members of their families, and respecting them is part of the fabric of our societies. What's more, it would be strange if this weren't so.[15] It would be odd, for example, to find parents going through the process of pregnancy and childbirth only to view their offspring as eligible menu items. These considerations—and many others like them—would not apply to space aliens discovering a world in which all humans had severe cognitive limitations. But they do apply *to us* in a world where severely cognitively disabled humans live in intimate relationships with non-disabled people. Such details might help explain why it makes sense for us to show a level of respect toward our fellow humans that we don't typically show animals, even if the individuals in question lack the characteristics that underlie humans' moral status more generally.

The preceding considerations provide a basis for denying that our judgments in the space alien example reflect how *we* ought to treat severely cognitively disabled humans. But are these arguments decisive? It's open to vegetarians to deny this. For instance, they might worry that facts about human psychology and family relations cannot tell us what would be wrong with a society that *did not* care about its severely cognitively disabled members and decided to farm them for food.[16] Given their complaints about discrimination, we should also not be surprised to find vegetarians insisting our partiality toward our fellow humans manifests precisely the "speciesist" prejudice they've been trying to uproot.

Concerns like these demand more attention than I can give them here. However, to see the bottom line, we need to ask: what would be the upshot of denying that we can distinguish between our judgments about the aliens example and our own attitudes and practices? Vegetarians who point to the overlaps between humans' and animals' cognitive traits encourage us to think that eliminating our partiality toward severely cognitively disabled humans would imply showing animals the same level of consideration we currently show our disabled relatives. But our earlier discussion suggests the more plausible upshot is in the opposite direction. If it's objectionably discriminatory to show our disabled relatives any more consideration than their inherent characteristics command, then that would seem to imply we should change our attitudes toward these humans, withdrawing from them the respect we currently consider appropriate.[17] The fact that this conclusion seems unacceptable provides at least some motivation for thinking it's desirable—and not wrongfully discriminatory—to show partiality toward severely cognitively disabled humans. But if that were not OK, it's far from obvious this would be a point in favor of the moral outlook the principled opponents of meat-eating seek to defend. Rather, it would seemingly recommend a view toward disabled humans that most of us find repugnant—and I think rightly so.

EATING OUR FELLOW CREATURES

In an important 1978 article,[18] Cora Diamond offers a powerful critique of the anti-meat arguments we've been discussing—not from a meat-eater's perspective, but rather from a vegetarian one. Her objection goes like this. When defenders of animal rights try to explain what's wrong with eating meat, they focus on all the ways *raising and killing* animals for food is analogous to raising and killing severely cognitively disabled humans for the same purpose. However, the issue of raising and killing is largely beside the point, for we find it objectionable to eat humans even when there's no raising or killing involved. *"We do not eat our dead,"* she writes, "even when they have died in automobile accidents or been struck by lightning, and their flesh might be first class."[19] Likewise, she observes, vegetarians typically consider it inappropriate to eat animals even when their treatment in life was unobjectionable. Eating a deer would still be repellent to them even if it had died in an automobile accident or lightning storm.[20] In Diamond's view, a full explanation of the vegetarian outlook needs to account for this basic conviction that animals are simply *not the sorts of things to be eaten,* just as meat-eaters and vegetarians alike regard humans as *non-food.*

For her part, Diamond holds back from attempting a decisive defense of this vegetarian conviction.[21] But to begin to make sense of it, she observes that many of us are brought up with (at least) two very different ways of thinking about animals. On the one hand, there is a mental schema according to which animals are means to our dietary ends—chicken breasts, pork chops, and hamburgers in the process of coming into existence. On the other hand, there exists equally another schema according to which animals are our "fellow creatures"—the sorts of beings we might take into our homes and nurse back to health if we found one injured on our lawn, or for which we might hang a feeder to entice a visit. Diamond rightly observes that when we think of animals as "fellow creatures," it doesn't come naturally to view them as food. When watching a bird at the feeder, for example, one doesn't typically think: "I wonder if there's enough meat on that one for a good snack."

Diamond's suggestion is that when vegetarians urge us to refrain from eating animals, this latter mentality at least partly drives their thinking. Rather than viewing animals as foodstuffs, they think we should appreciate more fully that these are our fellow creatures, generalizing a mindset we already apply to many other animals in our day-to-day lives. Diamond points out that if we took on such a mindset, this would mean coming to see animals as not the sorts of things to be eaten—just as we already think of our fellow humans this way.

For the sake of discussion, let's suppose Diamond's account captures how some vegetarians think about animals and why they're uncomfortable with eating meat—all meat—regardless of how it's obtained. Let's likewise suppose vegetarians and meat-eaters alike are familiar with viewing animals in certain contexts as "fellow creatures" that are not naturally regarded as food (e.g., wildlife, pets). For our purposes, the crucial question for our purposes is whether meat-eaters make a moral mistake if they continue thinking of certain animals in certain contexts as eligible to be eaten (e.g., farm animals raised for food) instead of generalizing the "fellow creatures" mindset.

As Diamond recognizes, the answer to this question can't be based simply on the fact that people are thinking and acting differently in some contexts than others. For there are many contexts in which people sensibly think and act differently from how they do elsewhere. For example, we might generally think of our fellow humans as not the sorts of things to be sliced open with a knife, but surgeons properly adopt a different mindset in the operating room. Likewise, we normally view other people as not the sorts of things to be punched in the face for fun, but this mentality doesn't apply in a boxing gym. If there's a problem with viewing animals as "fellow creatures" in some contexts and "food" in others, it can't simply be that these attitudes are different from one another. There has to be something deeper to explain why the outlook which treats animals as food items is objectionable.

Reflecting on our attitudes toward eating other humans helps clarify what would be needed for Diamond's case to go through. Most of us think part of what it means to respect people is ascribing them a special significance—what we might call a "dignity"—that would be contradicted if we viewed them as eligible to be eaten.[22] The problem isn't just that eating humans is harmful to them since, as we've seen, there are many ways to eat people without harming them (e.g., after they've died from natural causes). Rather, the issue is that respecting a person's dignity involves seeing them a particular way, and viewing them as food is at odds with that mentality. A surgeon doesn't negate her patient's dignity by cutting her open in the operating room, and a boxer doesn't negate her opponent's dignity by punching her in the ring. But someone who views another person's body as food exhibits an attitude toward that person which is incompatible with respecting her dignity—or so many people seem to believe.

Of course, it's fair to ask *why* we think eating people's bodies is at odds with respecting their dignity. In truth, I'm not sure there's a good answer to this question. Certainly, there have been cultures in which people eat human flesh, and some of these cultures have regarded the act of eating a dead person as not disrespectful but venerating. There are various *practical* reasons for not eating dead people, especially having to do with the dangerous illnesses that may have killed them in the first place. But once we bracket these pragmatic considerations and ask whether there's anything *intrinsically* undignified about having one's body eaten after one's death, we may ultimately have to concede this connection between indignity and being eaten is simply a cultural artifact.[23]

Let's put aside that puzzle for the moment, however, and take for granted that viewing people as food conflicts with respecting their dignity. The key question for us is whether viewing animals as food is problematic in an analogous way.[24] Unfortunately for Diamond's account, there are good reasons to be skeptical of this. Virtually all of us—including vegetarians—accept that animals are the sorts of things that can properly be eaten in at least some contexts. In particular, we tend to see animals this way when we're thinking about the natural ecological relationships in which wild animals exist. Nonhuman animals are food for predators, food for scavengers, and food for decomposers. Whereas we'd be mortified at the sight of a *person* (or even a corpse) being torn to pieces by a pride of lions, we tend not to be troubled when the same fate befalls other animals. (Those of us who find it uncomfortable to watch animals eat one another tend to interpret this as a product of *our* delicate sensibilities rather than anything inherently unbecoming about animal flesh being eaten.) When we view other animals in their roles as members of natural ecosystems, it seems clear to us animals *are* food—they *are* the sorts of things that are eligible to be eaten.

This ecological outlook does contrast with the attitudes we sometimes take toward "fellow creatures" in daily life. Diamond is right that we don't typically regard animals as food when we see them around the neighborhood. But my sense is that if these two attitudes ever come into tension, most of us more readily abandon the "fellow creature" mind-set than the one which views animals as edible ecosystem participants. When I watch a blue jay terrorize the other birds at the feeder, I don't see it as the sort of thing to be eaten. But I would quickly shake off this perspective if a Cooper's hawk swooped down and made the blue jay into its lunch.

Notice again how different this is from how we think about our fellow human beings. If we saw a crocodile capture a person on the banks of a river, we wouldn't shrug our shoulders and say, "Oh well, I suppose we're all ultimately food for something else!" Most of us hold a deep visceral conviction that a person is not the sort of thing to be eaten. (Some people hold this view so deeply that they find it unsettling to think of worms decomposing bodies in coffins.) On the other hand, when it comes to animals we regard as our "fellow creatures," this mentality seems much less firmly held, and we often abandon it as soon as animals' ecological roles are made salient. Human beings *are not food*, but other animals are.

It's worth noting that some vegetarians find it discomfiting that wild animals eat one another and wish we could eliminate predation without undermining ecological functioning.[25] This viewpoint has occasionally brought animal rights perspectives into the crosshairs of environmentalists, who see such ideas as anathema to a proper appreciation of the natural world.[26] For our purposes, however, these tensions are beside the point. I take it that even vegetarians who lament the existence of predation would grant that if a wild animal died from natural causes, it would be fine for vultures to descend upon its corpse and tear into it for their dinner. The key point is that, in adopting such an outlook, they take a view toward the animal's corpse that's dramatically different from the one we typically take toward human beings. Most people who saw vultures descending upon a human corpse would think it proper to try to shoo them away—ecological functioning be damned.

This example helps to clarify the kind of outlook that would be required for Diamond's argument to go through. Diamond is inviting us to change the way we think about animals—what animals mean to us, our outlooks on the sorts of things they are. When it comes to human beings, most of us think people are not the sorts of things to be eaten. Even if a person were impeccably treated during her life and died from natural causes, it would still seem inappropriate to eat her corpse—because humans are not food. Likewise, most of us would recoil at allowing the corpse to be torn to pieces by lions, crocodiles, or vultures—not because the animals would be doing anything wrong; again, simply because of a visceral sense that humans are not food. Although Diamond invites us likewise to regard animals as not the sorts of things to be eaten, anyone with an ecological understanding will recognize animals very much are the sorts of things to be eaten. To the extent this is correct, the particular significance and meaning Diamond invites us to assign to animals seems tenuous. At the very least, it does not seem like the sort of outlook we could condemn a person for not adopting.

On the reverse side of the coin, some readers may feel pulled by this discussion to move in the opposite direction, dispensing with the idea that there's anything wrong with wild animals treating humans as food. After all, such a world-view seems to place humans outside the natural order, implying a kind of exceptional status that also lies in tensions with our ecological understandings. In this connection, after being attacked and nearly killed by a crocodile, the Australian eco-feminist philosopher Val Plumwood remarked:

> Large predators like lions and crocodiles present an important test for us. An ecosystem's ability to support large predators is a mark of its ecological integrity. Crocodiles and other creatures that can take human life also present a test of our ecological identity. When they're allowed to live freely, these creatures indicate our preparedness to coexist with the otherness of the earth, and to recognize ourselves in mutual, ecological terms, as part of the food chain, eaten as well as eater.[27]

Views like Plumwood's are provocative, to say the least. But as we contemplate their merits, we find ourselves once again heading down a path that cannot help vegetarians' case. Diamond's purpose was to highlight that, just as we tend to think there's something wrong with viewing humans as food, vegetarians tend to extend a similar attitude to animals, likewise regarding them as not the sorts of things to be eaten. Plumwood's observations raise the possibility that, upon further reflection, we may conclude that our discomfort toward viewing humans as food is on a weaker footing than we realized. But rather than showing animals possess the same dignity we ascribe to human beings, this line of reasoning would only push us to question our attitudes of reverence toward one another.

There is one last vegetarian argument I want to examine in this chapter which, like the one we just finished discussing, doesn't focus on how food animals are raised. Jeff McMahan has perceptively observed that, regardless of how farmers treat their livestock, all modern forms of meat production involve killing animals before the end of their natural lifespans. Insofar as living out a full life is good for animals, killing them impairs their interests by depriving them of the valuable opportunity to go on living. If we take animals' interests seriously, McMahan reasons, we should regard these deprivations as justifiable only in the name of serving powerful interests. But as we discussed in the previous chapter, virtually none of us gets enough value from our chicken breasts, pork chops, or hamburgers to overbalance the sacrifices imposed on the animals we eat. Thus, McMahan concludes it's typically wrong to kill animals for food.[28]

In arguing for this conclusion, McMahan doesn't deny the possibility of "humane" farming. He's willing to grant, for example, that it may be possible to raise and kill animals without causing them serious discomfort, suffering, or fear. Nor does McMahan resort to controversial claims about animal cognition. He refrains from appealing to the ideas that animals consciously *desire* to live out their lives or that killing them would frustrate crucial long-term projects in which they're engaged.[29] For McMahan, the issue is simply that it's *good for animals* to live out a full life (assuming they're treated humanely), and an early death means losing out on this valuable opportunity.

In evaluating McMahan's position, let's grant for the sake of discussion that he's right about where the balance of interests lies between meat-eaters and the animals they eat. If we consider the lifetime wellbeing animals lose from being killed, we'll rarely find meat-eaters who benefit more than this amount from consuming their flesh.[30] But does this mean it's wrong to kill animals for food? The answer is unclear for two main reasons.

The first source of difficulties has to do with the moral significance of the interests McMahan brings to light. In this chapter, we've already seen that our duty to honor an interest is not always determined by its strength. Recalling our earlier examples, my stronger interest in using your watercolors doesn't obligate you to let me have them. Likewise, although you may not steal even a tiny sum of my money, it may nevertheless be acceptable for you to bankrupt me as a competitor in the marketplace even if my losses would outweigh any benefits you would achieve. As a general matter, the fact that something affects someone's interests is only indirectly related to what (if anything) we're obligated to do. Sometimes we're duty-bound to make big sacrifices to honor weak interests, and sometimes we're permitted to create major setbacks for others in pursuit of comparatively minor aims of our own.

What's more, the strengths of our reasons to defer to others' interests often link to precisely the kinds of considerations McMahan leaves aside when he sets up his argument. For instance, when neglecting your interests would cause you discomfort, suffering, or fear, this would seem to provide particularly strong reasons to ensure your interests are honored. If your lifelong aspirations or projects hung in the balance with respect to a particular choice of mine, that too would strengthen my case for acting in deference to you. Mutual participation in cooperative schemes can generate still further reasons for sacrifice. If you and I were involved in a community in which each of us could expect members to make sacrifices for others' benefits, this system of reciprocity could provide us with powerful reasons to promote each other's interests at our own expense.

However, we've seen that McMahan has given up appealing to considerations like these in presenting his argument. His point is not that killing animals for food inflicts negative mental states upon them, frustrates their projects, or violates any terms of cooperation. Rather, it's simply that killing animals before their time causes them not to get something that would be good for them. At least on its face, it's not obvious this interest, divorced from all the factors McMahan has agreed to set aside, can generate the kind of binding moral obligation needed to justify his conclusion.

To illustrate the problem in an admittedly glib way, imagine you learn that, if you spend time with your friends this afternoon (which you desire to do), this will cause me to miss out on a set of experiences which would benefit me. To be clear: seeing your friends would not cause me to have negative experiences—it's not that I'd feel bad if you saw them, only that I'd be deprived of certain benefits I might otherwise have enjoyed. The benefits in question are not intimately connected to my projects or aspirations; in fact, I've never so much as contemplated them, and it would be false to say I desire or expect you to avoid seeing your friends for my sake. It's also not the case that deferring to my interests would contribute to a reciprocal scheme of cooperation in which you and I are participants. In fact, I'm not much of a reciprocator or cooperator to begin with, and there's no chance you or anyone else would ever be in a position to benefit from me sacrificing my interests like you're now considering sacrificing yours. In a case like this, it seems reasonable to wonder: is it really obligatory to sacrifice your interests for my sake and stay home? Or is it OK in such a scenario to say, "I see you stand to lose if I decide to spend time with my friends, but that's just too bad for you"? In my view, the latter response would be entirely valid.

We need to be careful about inferring too much from an example such as this. Animals aren't simply thoughtless, unco-operative people; they're different kinds of beings entirely. The point of the example is simply to reinforce the point that, once we introduce all the caveats McMahan is willing to grant, it's no longer obvious that raising animals humanely and killing them for food represents a failure to consider their interests adequately. McMahan is right that slaughtering animals before their time deprives them of an opportunity to get something that would be good for them. But it's not as clear as he seems to think that this is a type of loss we have a duty not to create.

A second difficulty for McMahan's position comes from the fact that, in typical farming operations, animals are only in a position to live *at all* because farmers intend to kill them. Farmers breed and raise animals specifically for their meat. Once the animals exist, it would obviously be better from the animals' standpoint not to be eaten and instead live out their lives under the farmers' care. But in practice, this latter option is not meaningfully on the table. Farmers' choice is between producing meat or taking up a different line of work, not between producing meat and raising farm animals as pets.

Some meat-eaters have pointed to this fact to argue that it's positively *desirable* to produce meat since failing to do so would consign many animals to nonexistence.[31] Animals treated as conscientious omnivores demand would presumably live quite good—albeit abbreviated—lives. It might seem worse never to be born than to live such a short, pleasant life. Yet,

McMahan reasonably questions whether we can meaningfully compare the "goodness" or "badness" of existence to that of nonexistence.[32] Even if eliminating meat production would dramatically reduce the number of farm animals born, it seems sensible to doubt whether the loss of these merely possible lives would represent a moral tragedy.

The important question for us, however, is not whether it's *morally essential* to produce meat. The question is whether meat production is *morally wrong*. If it turns out that raising and killing animals for food is morally *neutral*—say, because we can't meaningfully compare it to the alternative of abstaining— then we should have no objection to farmers and meat-eaters doing as they wish.

It might seem like if we reject the possibility of meaningfully comparing farm animals' lives at the hands of "conscientious omnivores" to the alternative in which they're never born, then this would seal the case in favor of conscientious omnivorism. Even if they couldn't say it's *better* to have the animals exist than not exist, conscientious omnivores could at least say it's *not worse* to have them exist, and hence it's OK to take that option. However, McMahan denies the morally relevant comparison is between *the overall practice* of raising animals for food and never breeding them in the first place. As he sees it, there are multiple distinct actions involved in raising animals for meat, and these need to be assessed individually rather than together. "It can be permissible to bring about a series of effects through a single act," he writes, "and yet not be permissible to bring about each of the effects through a series of acts."[33] At the moment when a farmer is deciding whether or not to kill an animal, McMahan contends, *that* action needs to be evaluated on its independent merits, for "the permissibility of individual acts is determined by the considerations that favor them at the time of action and cannot be derived from the desirability of the larger practices in which they are embedded."[34]

McMahan's discomfort with justifying actions by appealing to overarching practices is idiosyncratic in the moral philosophy literature.[35] In countless domains, and for countless different reasons, we make such appeals to vindicate countless actions which might otherwise seem unmotivated or even wrong. We may illustrate this diversity of practice-based appeals by considering some examples. Why should a person have to pay a hefty fine just for blocking a fire hydrant when no fire was occurring? Why should courts uphold a contract that was foolish for the parties to enter? Why should a likely murderer be set free just because there's reasonable doubt about their guilt? Why should a batter be declared "out" just because they've accumulated three strikes? The answer in each case comes from considering the overarching practice in which the action in question is embedded. If McMahan hopes to persuade us that practice-based appeals are generally inadmissible as moral justifications, he faces an uphill battle.[36]

In addition to representing a radical revision of our ordinary moral thinking, McMahan's arguments also yield implications for the debate over meat-eating that seem frankly bizarre. In particular, McMahan's arguments suggest that if farmers could raise and kill animals *without* undertaking multiple distinct actions, this could be OK: his fundamental issue with humane meat production is simply that more than one step is involved. McMahan explains, for example, that it would be acceptable on his view to produce meat by creating "a breed of animals genetically programmed to die at a comparatively early age, when their meat would taste best."[37] It would seem similarly compatible with his arguments to automate meat production so that, once the process was set in motion, animals were raised and killed by machines without further human intervention.[38] In both of these cases, no human actions would be taken that sacrificed the interests of animals that already existed, and so McMahan's concerns would not apply.

I'm aware incredulity is a poor substitute for a carefully formulated argument. However, it seems strange to think the fatal moral problem with humane meat production is that it can't yet be carried out through a single action and must be broken into multiple steps. It seems especially strange to formulate such an argument around the idea that only a process involving a single human intervention could account adequately for animals' interests in living out their lives. If our concern is whether animals have beneficial experiences, we should seemingly ascribe moral equivalence to practices that raise and kill them through genetic engineering, full automation, and conventional slaughter—assuming the animals experience equivalent lives. Although McMahan may bite the bullet and insist it makes a major difference how we break apart these processes, ethical vegetarians should consider whether they're best served by building their position around such claims.

Ultimately, McMahan is correct that killing animals before their time impairs their interests by depriving them of the opportunity to live a full life. But as we've seen, it's hard to draw a straightforward connection between this fact and the wrongness of killing animals for food. For one thing, it's not clear these are the kinds of losses we have an obligation not to cause. Matters are muddied further by the fact that the animals wouldn't exist if not for their handlers' intentions to kill them. These complications make it doubtful that the deprivations McMahan identifies reflect a deep moral problem with producing meat the way conscientious omnivores advocate.

For his part, McMahan thinks it tells particularly clearly against "eating animals the nice way" that we wouldn't countenance treating humans in a similar fashion—even if those humans exhibited severe cognitive disabilities that limited them to the same levels of functioning as animals.[39] We've seen in this chapter, however, that our treatment of cognitively disabled humans is special in ways that go beyond these individuals' intrinsic characteristics. Indeed, as Cora Diamond has helped us see, our attitudes toward eating humans are more stringent than even McMahan's account can capture. We wouldn't consider it appropriate to raise our fellow humans for food even if they were allowed to live out their natural lives in the way McMahan's account demands. These attitudes are special, however, rooted in our distinctive affinities toward other human beings. Although some vegetarians might not agree with these attitudes, we've seen that rejecting them would provide little help to McMahan's position. Debunking them would only push us toward a view McMahan considers "so deeply repugnant that it need not be explored in depth": that severely cognitively disabled humans deserve a level of consideration no greater than we presently ascribe to animals.[40]

THE POSSIBILITY OF "CONSCIENTIOUS OMNIVORISM"

The core thesis of ethical vegetarianism is that it's wrong to eat meat. Many arguments for this claim revolve around how the vast majority of meat is currently produced, using practices that seem cruel, inequitable, unsustainable, and unsafe. However, these arguments don't show it's wrong to eat meat *as such*, for it seems possible to get around them by adopting better practices. Self-described "conscientious omnivores" point to this possibility to reject vegetarians' core ethical thesis, arguing that eating meat is OK when it's produced according to rigorous moral standards.

To refute the conscientious omnivore's position, vegetarians would need arguments that show it's wrong *in principle* to eat meat—even if it were produced humanely, equitably, sustainably, and safely.[41] In this chapter, we've considered several arguments along these lines and found all of them wanting:

- Against the view that animals' moral status should be seen as equal to our own, I argued that preserving the core ethical notion of *respect* requires us to appeal to characteristics only humans have, such as our capacities for living integrated, meaningful lives and for moral cooperation.

- Against the view that it's "speciesist" to distinguish between the level of consideration animals are due and that which we ought to show toward severely cognitively disabled humans, I argued it's morally acceptable for us to show partiality toward our fellow humans—and rejecting this claim would only yield the unpalatable upshot that we should downgrade the status we ascribe our severely disabled relatives.

- Against the view that we should regard animals as inherently *not the sorts of things to be eaten*, I argued a sophisticated appreciation of the ecological role of nonhuman animals creates major obstacles to a worldview according to which animals *are not food*.

- Against the view that it's wrong to deprive farm animals of their interests in living their full natural lives, I raised doubts about whether these interests give rise to genuine moral duties, especially given that the relevant alternative to killing these animals for food is for them not to exist in the first place.

If the arguments of this chapter have been on target, then the core thesis of ethical vegetarianism is on shaky ground. Conscientious omnivores can plausibly argue eating meat is *only* problematic because of how it's typically produced, and if animals were raised and killed humanely, equitably, sustainably, and safely, there would be nothing wrong with eating them. If this conclusion is granted—and of course, vegetarians may still debate whether it should be—then this yields an initial affirmative response to our core question of whether it's OK to eat meat. Whereas ethical vegetarians insist the answer is a flat "No," we've now seen grounds for thinking a better answer is "At least in some cases, it could be."

This, however, is a highly limited conclusion. For in the real world, nearly all the animals we eat are treated in ways conscientious omnivores condemn. As I said in Chapter 1, my goal in this book is not to show that *we can imagine cases* where it's OK to eat meat. Rather, my task is to build the case for thinking it's OK to eat the meat that's readily available in supermarkets and restaurants, as most meat-eaters do. Establishing this further conclusion is much harder than showing that it's possible to justify eating meat from producers who behave far more scrupulously than is common in reality. Thus, let us now turn to this more difficult challenge.

Three

In the previous chapter, I made a case for thinking that if animals were raised humanely, equitably, sustainably, and safely, then eating them would be morally OK. That conclusion challenged the core thesis of ethical vegetarianism by showing it's not *inherently* wrong to eat meat. However, even if you buy the arguments in that chapter, this would be an exceedingly narrow victory since meat production in today's marketplace virtually always raises serious concerns about animals, workers, the environment, and public health. If we want to eat meat "in the regular way," we can't be satisfied with saying it *could be* OK to eat meat if it were produced with meticulous care. We have to ask whether it's still OK to eat it even when it's *not* produced in ways we can conscientiously endorse.[1]

The rest of this book tackles this more challenging question. I set the stage in this chapter by examining the problems affecting the meat industry's operations. In the chapters that follow, I'll explain why it's hard to draw a straight line from the existence of these problems to our obligations as consumers—in other words, why even if critics are right to oppose many of the industry's practices, that doesn't prove it's wrong

DOI: 10.4324/9781003221944-3

to eat meat. Regardless of how we settle that issue, however, we shouldn't ignore the fact that the meat industry is a source of serious problems that deserve to be addressed. For now, let's focus on understanding the problems as they are, setting aside for later the question of what these problems mean for whether it's OK to eat meat.

Before launching in, it's worth noting that a truly comprehensive overview of meat industry practices would require a lengthy book in itself. For the sake of brevity, I'll focus on the most common practices used to produce chicken, pork, and beef in the United States. This will mean leaving out a number of important things, including many other types of meat production (e.g., turkey, lamb, fish, shellfish), animal products that are not meat (e.g., dairy, eggs, leather, honey), and practices used in other countries or by specific groups in America (e.g., religious slaughter). These omissions imply you should not rely on the following discussion for all your information about the meat industry. (Frankly, that seems like common sense anyway.) But a narrowed focus will suit this book's purpose for two main reasons. First, the practices I cover will include many of those considered most clearly objectionable by critics of meat-eating: whereas some ethical vegetarians make exceptions for things like seafood, eggs, and dairy, virtually all agree people should not eat chicken, pork, or beef as mainstream American companies produce it. Second, the practices I discuss provide ample illustration of vegetarians' concerns regarding the meat industry's cruel, exploitative, unsustainable, and dangerous practices. It thus seems plausible that if I can show it's OK to eat ordinary chicken, pork, and beef in the United States despite the issues covered in this chapter, then similar arguments will help us see why it's OK to consume other meat and animal products as well.[2]

In the United States, a meat chicken (known in the industry as a "broiler") generally begins its life on a breeding farm. As an egg, it's collected from its mother and incubated under carefully controlled conditions until it hatches. After hatching, it's sorted by sex, vaccinated, counted, and placed in a basket for delivery to a growing farm. At its new home, the broiler chick is placed in a rearing house alongside thousands of others of the same age, where it spends the next few weeks eating and drinking its way to marketable weight. When the desired weight is reached, the chicken is captured by a catching crew, loaded into a truck, and taken to a processing plant (i.e., a slaughterhouse).[3] There, it's hung upside down by its feet, submerged in a water bath, and rendered unconscious (i.e., "stunned") with an electric shock. (Some plants use other methods, like knocking out chickens with carbon dioxide.) The unconscious chicken's throat is slit by a rotating blade, and it's allowed to bleed out. Then its feathers are removed, its feet are cut off, and its insides are emptied out. Finally, the chicken's carcass is cleaned, inspected, and chilled for its trip off to market.[4]

Welfare concerns can arise at many points in this process—more than I can hope to list.[5] For purposes of illustration, I'll mention just a few. If chicks are born with illnesses or health defects, they're typically killed.[6] This is most commonly done by "maceration," which basically amounts to being placed in a high-speed grinder. When done correctly, this results in near-instantaneous death, but mistakes and equipment malfunctions can yield gruesome results.[7] When chicks are transported from breeding farms to growing houses, they're sometimes exposed to temperature extremes that can stress and even kill them.[8]

At growing farms, chickens are housed in buildings that are essentially barren except for food and water lines. These buildings become increasingly crowded as the occupants grow, and conditions inside them are often harsh. Despite efforts to maintain air quality, dust poses a persistent challenge, and the accumulation of moisture and waste can lead to high concentrations of ammonia that irritates chickens' throats and lungs and damages the skin on their breasts and feet.[9] Chickens in growing houses are also vulnerable to outbreaks of infection by parasites and other pathogens.[10]

The chickens commonly used in American farming operations have been bred for rapid growth. This has drastically increased farmers' output, but these fast-growing chickens are susceptible to a variety of chronic diseases, skeletal disorders, and motor dysfunctions.[11] Exacerbating these problems is the fact that chickens can be made to eat and grow even faster by raising them in artificially lit environments that encourage them to stay awake.[12] Although taking advantage of this can negatively impact birds' welfare, the prospect of increased profits can give farmers a perverse incentive to induce faster growth than is optimal for chickens' health.

When market-weight chickens are ready to be sent off for processing, catching crews often cause serious injuries, and the rigors of travel can kill birds en route to the processing plant.[13] Chickens at the plant can be injured as they're loaded onto the stunning apparatus,[14] and mistakes in the stunning process can lead to chickens being killed while still conscious.[15] If errors compound seriously enough, a chicken can even find itself trapped alive in a machine designed to scald its feathers away with boiling water.[16]

As we'll discuss in more detail below, all major chicken producers take measures to mitigate outcomes like these.

However, although these efforts reduce the rates of problems, they don't eliminate them completely. Every producer expects to see some level of mortality, illness, and injury in the course of raising and processing chickens for market. According to the National Chicken Council, around 5% of chickens die prematurely on American farms.[17] And in an industry that raises more than nine billion birds per year in the United States alone,[18] even low error rates can lead to the mishandling of thousands if not millions of birds.

Alongside these concerns about the treatment of chickens, the broiler industry is also criticized for its treatment of workers. The American chicken industry is dominated by companies that control all aspects of production, from raising to slaughtering to marketing (known as "vertical integration"). Despite their massive influence, these companies don't typically carry out the day-to-day activities of raising chickens themselves. Instead, they enter into contracts with independent farmers who breed, grow, and slaughter according to the company's specifications.[19]

The people who run these contract operations earn a nominally decent income, bringing in an average household income of $68,445 in 2011 (compared to $50,504 for the median household in the nation).[20] However, these numbers conceal important sources of financial risk and uncertainty facing many chicken growers. Establishing a grow-out operation requires a substantial up-front investment, with typical startup costs around $1 million.[21] These investments are typically financed through debt, with growers on the hook for significant bank payments to keep their operations afloat.[22] However, on the income side of the ledger, contract growers are generally not assured a specific rate in exchange for their services. Instead, the fees they get for their output are dependent on how their operations perform, not just in absolute terms but also relative to other growers working for their company.[23] If things don't turn out as planned, growers can find themselves on the hook for hundreds of thousands of dollars of debt with little means of repayment.

The employees who work for these contract growers experience significant hardships as well. If you're an entry-level chicken catcher (i.e., someone who catches and loads chickens into crates for transportation to slaughter) or a worker in a processing plant, you can expect to earn around $22,000 per year.[24] Jobs like these aren't just poorly paid: they also expose workers to harsh conditions. In chicken houses, catch crews often breathe the same air as the chickens, inhaling substantial concentrations of irritating dust, ammonia, and bacterial endotoxins.[25] In processing plants, line workers work long hours performing repetitive motions that leave them mentally exhausted and with chronic pain in their hands, arms, shoulders, and backs.[26] The inherently difficult nature of their work is made even more challenging by the rapid speeds at which they're expected to process animals moving through the plant.[27] And working elbow to elbow with dozens of other workers means processing plant employees are especially vulnerable to illness. In just the first few months of the COVID-19 pandemic of 2020, for example, viral outbreaks in meat and poultry facilities affected thousands of workers across 23 states, serving as a key early conduit for the virus' spread.[28]

In theory, occupational health and safety regulations limit how bad things can get for chicken industry workers. In reality, however, many report feeling too intimidated to report abuses.[29] In particular, a large proportion of processing plant workers are undocumented immigrants who fear deportation if they stand up for their rights.[30] In cases where workers have tried to organize for better treatment, their efforts have often been harshly rebuked. Some companies have shut down plants where employees attempted to unionize, only to quickly reopen with different workers. Other employers have resorted to more direct forms of intimidation, interrogating workers about union sympathies and threatening to penalize or fire anyone daring to organize.[31]

In addition to its questionable treatment of animals and workers, modern chicken farming can also produce serious environmental impacts. If chicken manure is managed poorly, it can wash into rivers and lakes, contributing to bacterial contamination and algae blooms that kill fish, ruin recreation, and create health risks such as "blue baby syndrome."[32] Chicken farms can also produce bad smells that bother neighbors and lower property values. In well-run operations, strong odors are short-lived, occurring mainly when chicken houses are cleaned out or when manure is spread as fertilizer.[33] However, in cases where poor management allows excess moisture to accumulate, the same buildup of ammonia that undermines air quality inside the houses can produce powerful smells outside them.

The crowded, warm, and humid conditions inside chicken houses can also make them virtual petri dishes for disease. Some chicken producers combat these dangers with prophylactic doses of certain medicines, including antibiotics, but these practices help keep chickens healthier only at the risk of allowing diseases to become resistant over time. Disease threats are obviously worrisome from the standpoint of animal welfare, but of added concern is the possibility of chicken illnesses mutating in ways that make them dangerous to humans. Such mutations have occurred in the past (for example, in the case of "bird flu"), and industry critics say it's only a matter of time before major outbreaks happen again.[34]

To its credit, the poultry industry has taken measures to mitigate many impacts of chicken farming on the environment and public health. In some cases, these efforts have been driven by federal regulations. For example, the US Environmental Protection Agency has used the Clean Water Act to limit farmers' ability to pollute waterways with runoff,[35] and it is investigating the need to bring the Clean Air Act to bear in controlling ammonia and other pollutants.[36] In other cases, industry players have collaborated voluntarily with government agencies to reduce risks. For example, the US Department of Agriculture's Animal and Plant Health Inspection Service works with growers to protect their chickens from infectious diseases,[37] and major chicken producers employ strict biosecurity protocols to prevent people from accidentally bringing diseases into and out of chicken houses. Some companies have gone further. For example, many have phased out antibiotics except when ordered by veterinary caregivers.[38] Some have made ambitious pledges to reduce carbon emissions and water use and to responsibly steward land used to grow chicken feed.[39] Measures like these go partway to addressing critics' concerns about the environmental and public health risks associated with chicken farming, but they don't prevent every danger. Chicken farms continue to be an important source of water and air pollution, and the crowded conditions of modern chicken houses create health hazards that producers cannot completely eliminate.

When we combine the preceding concerns about the chicken industry's treatment of its animals and workers, its impacts on the environment, and its threats to public health, we can see why vegetarians devote so much attention to how chickens are actually raised and killed. Even if it were morally blameless to eat chicken that was produced humanely, equitably, sustainably, and safely, this wouldn't entail it's OK to eat the vast majority of chicken we encounter in our day-to-day lives. To justify eating most actual chicken, we need to face up to all the ways chicken farming falls short of these ideals.

PORK

Detailing the pork industry's practices is made challenging by the lack of uniformity in how pigs are raised. Until relatively recently, most American pigs were owned by small-scale farms that combined raising animals with producing crops—typically corn or soybeans. Over the last few decades, however, the hog industry has consolidated considerably, and many of the largest producers now operate on different, more intensive models. In particular, whereas it was once normal for a pig to spend its entire life on a single small farm, it's more common today for pigs to split time between multiple specialized facilities, with some focusing on the early stages of life and others on the later stages.[40] I'll try in this section to provide a general sketch of the range of practices in the pork industry. In some places, I'll brush over minor details to prioritize ease of understanding over exhaustiveness. But I hope my simplified account will be enough to show that pork production raises many of the same kinds of ethical issues we saw in the discussion of chicken above.

The story of a typical American pig begins with its mother. A breeding sow is generally housed in either a group pen with other sows or in a metal stall on its own.[41] When she's ready to give birth, the sow is moved to a "farrowing crate" where she lies on the ground beneath a mechanism that holds her in place. (The purpose of this apparatus is to prevent the sow from accidentally crushing her piglets as she moves around.)[42] Here, she will lie while her piglets suckle and grow.

After about three weeks, each piglet is weaned (i.e., separated from its mother) and moved into a barn with other piglets. Depending on the operation in question, this barn could be adjacent to the one where the piglet was born, or it could be in another state. From this point on, the piglet's job is to eat and grow as quickly as possible. A typical piglet weighs between 13 and 15 lbs at weaning, and it'll grow to around 280 lbs by the time it's about six months old.[43]

Once a pig reaches marketable weight, it's loaded into a truck and brought to a processing plant for slaughter. Upon arrival, the pig rests for an hour or more to calm down from the rigors of travel. (Stress hormones reduce meat quality in pigs, so processors must provide pigs time to relax before they're killed.) The pig is then loaded into a chamber that uses carbon dioxide to render it unconscious. (Some plants accomplish this via electric shock.) Once unconscious, the pig is killed, hung to bleed, lowered into a scalding tank, dehaired, singed with fire to kill surface pathogens and remove any remaining hairs, gutted, split in half, chilled, and cut into pieces for market.[44]

As with chickens, welfare problems can arise at many points in this process. Again, I'll relate just a few examples. To begin, the farrowing crates used to control sows during the birthing and suckling process are extremely restrictive, essentially pinning the animals in place for weeks at a time. Even when breeding sows are not farrowing, many producers confine them to stalls that offer very little space—often not even enough for them to turn around—and the animals live this way not just for a few weeks but for the bulk of their lives. These stalls facilitate monitoring the animals' food intake and physical health, but they do so only at a substantial cost to their ability to engage in natural pig activities.[45]

In their first weeks of life, piglets undergo several painful procedures to prepare them for adulthood. For example, male piglets are castrated to prevent them from developing the aggressive personality of an adult boar and from having their meat take on a bad odor and flavor known as "boar taint." In the United States, this procedure is typically done surgically without medication to dull the pain.[46]

Another controversial early-life procedure is known as "tail docking." When left to their own devices, pigs in mainstream farming operations often bite each other's tails—sometimes to drive other pigs away from desired resources such as food and sometimes to vent frustration due to stressors like heat, humidity, and chronic pain.[47] Tail-biting can produce serious injuries, and it can become self-reinforcing. Once a wound has been opened on a pig's tail, others will often become more interested in exploring and biting the tail for themselves.[48] Although providing pigs with more comfortable and stimulating environments can reduce tail-biting to some extent,[49] many producers control the problem further by removing all but a few centimeters of their piglets' tails from the outset. This "docking" of pigs' tails reduces the amount and severity of tail-biting. However, the procedure to shorten the tail is painful (especially when done without anesthetic), and tail docking can result in a nerve condition called a neuroma that makes the tip hypersensitive and susceptible to chronic pain.[50]

As with chickens, further welfare concerns can crop up throughout the period when a pig is growing to market weight and heading off to slaughter. However, one thing that sets pigs apart is their high level of intelligence, which translates to a much greater level of complexity in a pig's natural life. Like humans, young pigs in the wild undergo a lengthy developmental process that prepares them for adulthood. A piglet naturally spends around three months at its mother's side before weaning, and it generally lives its first year in a tight-knit family group with its mother, siblings, and other close relatives.[51] Adult pigs are naturally active, social, and curious, moving around large ranges in hierarchically organized groups and habitually rooting through the dirt in search of food.[52]

These facts inspire special concerns about how pigs are raised in the pork industry today. For example, the fact that pigs are separated from their mothers at three weeks—rather than three months—generates worries about their developmental wellbeing, with some studies finding significantly higher levels of aggression and digestive problems in early weaned piglets.[53] The barren, metal-floored pens of a typical growing barn also raise psychological problems for pigs. Without suitable environmental enrichments to hold their interest, pigs become bored and aggressive,[54] and stress is exacerbated when pigs are too crowded to explore.[55] Breeding sows are at particular risk of cognitive deprivation since, as we've seen, they're often confined to stalls barely larger than their bodies, especially during pregnancy and birthing.[56]

Like chicken production, the pork industry also generates concerns about worker equity, environmental impacts, and public health hazards. Pork industry workers face many of the same harsh working conditions as in the broiler industry. The large volume of excrement produced by pigs is also a significant source of environmental dangers. As pig manure is stored in "lagoons" to be broken down by anaerobic bacteria, it releases noxious gases like ammonia and hydrogen sulfide that produce powerful smells[57] and can exacerbate local health problems like asthma.[58] Particularly in regions subject to flooding, the lagoons also threaten to send massive quantities of manure into public waterways during severe weather events.[59] Pig farming likewise creates disease risks that threaten humans as well as animals. The global outbreak of "swine flu" in 2009 killed over 150,000 people in its first year,[60] and other deadly diseases such as trichinella[61] and MRSA—methicillin-resistant *Staphylococcus aureas*[62]—are also linked to pig farms.

As with the preceding discussion of chickens, these short pages don't exhaust the objections to how pigs are raised, but they illuminate wide-ranging concerns about animal welfare, worker equity, environmental impacts, and biosecurity. Again, it's important to note that regulators and pork producers have taken many steps to mitigate these problems, but they haven't completely resolved critics' concerns.

BEEF

The last few decades have seen chicken and pork production move in the direction of comprehensive control over the animals' lives, with chickens and pigs raised in crowded artificial environments from birth until death. Things are different with beef cows. A typical beef cow is born in an outdoor pasture and spends its first six to nine months alongside its mother. By the time it's weaned, the calf weighs between 400 and 700 lbs.[63]

What happens after weaning depends on the specific business model of the operation. Many calves will be auctioned off to "stockers" or "backgrounders" who move them to tracts of grazing land to continue to grow. Others will remain for a few more months on the farms where they were born.[64] And still others will be sent directly to a "feeder" to be finished for market.[65]

Ultimately, the vast majority of beef cows spend their last few months on feedlots where they eat a concentrated diet of grain (such as corn) to develop the rich marbling consumers desire. These feedlots vary in size, with around 95% of operations holding 1,000 or fewer cattle at a time. However, the 5% of operations with capacities over 1,000 handle more than 80% of cattle that pass through feedlots each year. 40% move through gargantuan feedlots with capacities of 32,000 or more.[66]

After four to six months on a feedlot, a cow will weigh upwards of 1,300 lbs,[67] at which point it's loaded into a truck and brought to a processing plant. After it arrives, the cow rests a few hours (again, to prevent poor meat quality from stress hormones). Then it's walked through a system of chutes to a chamber where it's killed. The killing is typically done with a tool called a captive bolt gun that uses pressurized gas (or a blank bullet cartridge) to fire a metal rod into the cow's brain. (It's a "captive" bolt because the rod doesn't fully leave the machine: it's retracted after each use to be fired again.) Once the cow is dead, it's hung and allowed to bleed; then it's skinned, gutted, split in half, chilled, and cut into pieces for market.[68]

As with the other animals we've discussed, welfare issues can arise throughout this process. The transportation of cattle, for example, can result in stress and injuries, and accidents during slaughtering can cause major suffering. Due to the relatively hands-off nature of typical cattle-raising practices, however, objections to the handling of cows tend to fixate on a handful of practices used at the beginning of their lives and on their last few months on feedlots.

Like piglets, young calves typically endure several painful procedures during their first months of life. For example, they're typically branded in an effort to mitigate cattle theft. Branding can be done in several ways, but the traditional hot-iron method remains standard.[69] To prevent cows from growing their natural sharp horns (which can endanger both handlers and other cattle), young cows' horn buds are destroyed. This, too, is usually done with a hot iron, but it can also be performed surgically or with caustic chemicals.[70] To stop male calves from developing into strong, aggressive, culinarily undesirable bulls, they are castrated, either surgically or by using an elastic band to cut off the blood supply to the scrotum and testes (which eventually shrivel up and fall off). Each of these practices inherently involves some discomfort, but critics direct special frustration toward the large proportion of American cattle farmers who conduct these procedures without anesthetic.[71]

Finishing operations attract even sterner critiques, particularly focusing on the grain-based diets most cattle are fed. Whereas cows' digestive systems are impressively well suited to processing grass, they're not as good at dealing with richer feeds like corn. As a result, grain-fed cattle often develop serious issues with excess acid in their digestive systems, sometimes even leading to a condition where their blood plasma becomes dangerously acidified.[72] (This is why some producers, consumers, and activists push for purely grass-fed beef.)

Feedlot finishing is also responsible for many of the environmental and biosecurity concerns raised against beef producers. In keeping with the preceding discussions of chickens and pigs, the control of cow manure can be a serious issue, and regulations exist to limit pollution from these facilities. The concentration of large numbers of cattle on feedlots also generates a significant potential for disease.

Whether or not they're confined to feedlots, however, cattle contribute in a distinctive way to environmental problems of a more global nature. Cows' guts produce a great deal of methane when they digest food, and cow manure releases nitrous oxide, both of which are potent greenhouse gases. Because of these emissions—along with others released while raising and processing cattle—beef production accounts for nearly 6% of all human greenhouse gas emissions.[73] (To put that figure in context, the entire livestock sector accounts for 14.5% of human greenhouse gas emissions—roughly on par with emissions from transportation. With dairy cattle responsible for another 3% of the total, cows are responsible for almost two-thirds of the sector's emissions.[74])

The fact that cows spend so much of their time grazing in open pastureland leads to other environmental problems. Many parts of the world have seen vast swaths of natural forest cleared to accommodate cattle grazing. In South America, for example, cattle ranching has driven around 80% of Amazon deforestation.[75] Even more land is used to grow the crops cows eat in feedlot operations. In a world where undeveloped wildlife habitat is increasingly scarce, the amount of land that continues to be cleared for cows merits serious attention.

WHAT SHOULD BE OUR STANDARDS?

The preceding discussion reveals a litany of concerns with the meat industry's practices. In contrast with the previous chapter's vision of raising and killing animals humanely, equitably, sustainably, and safely, this chapter shows there are powerful reasons to doubt the meat industry's deservingness of *any* of these characterizations. For some readers, this may be enough to show there's something seriously wrong with how most meat is produced. However, others may feel conflicted about what to conclude from this examination. For one thing, some may struggle to see how the problems we've been discussing are distinctive to meat production rather than just examples of broader imperfections in our society's governance. Perhaps meat industry workers have things rough, for example, but so do many of the people who produce our clothes, electronics, and even fruits and vegetables.[76] Likewise, meat production is hardly the only domain in which people worry about environmental impacts or public health threats. Do the issues we've been discussing prove the meat industry is a *special* source of problems, or do they simply reflect broad dissatisfaction with our workplace regulations, environmental policies, and public health protections?

Further, some readers may have trouble deciding what standards a company would need to meet to qualify as humane, equitable, sustainable, and safe. Obviously, it would be nice if every company could operate so that everyone and everything came away having experienced nothing but pleasure and gains. But in the real world, we must face the fact that every industry is liable to accidents, abuses, poor judgments, and imperfections.

The meat industry's treatment of animals provides a powerful illustration of how such ambiguities combine to challenge our judgments. If there's anything that sets the meat industry apart from other sources of problems in society, it would seem to be the industry's relationships with its animals. Whereas many industries face concerns about worker treatment, environmental impacts, and public health risks, the meat industry stands alone in its control over billions of animal lives each year. Yet what should be our standards for assessing the industry's treatment of animals? Even if we regard it as clearly problematic to impose undue hardships on chickens, pigs, and cows in the name of eating their bodies, what counts as adequately "humane" in the context of animal agriculture?

Consider in this connection a memorable chapter from Jonathan Safran Foer's book, *Eating Animals*, in which Foer grapples with the operations of Niman Ranch, a company specializing in what it calls "natural, sustainable, and humanely raised meats."[77] Upon getting to know Frank Niman and learning more about his operations, Foer discovers that Niman Ranch avoids the worst problems he discovered in his research on mainstream farming. But Foer still recoils at some of the discomforts Niman's animals experience. The cows at Niman Ranch are still branded, castrated, and disbudded, for example—although using procedures Foer considers "the best there are."[78] They still finish their lives on feedlots—although these, too, differ from the industry norm in virtue of their "smaller scale, lack of drugs, better feed, better upkeep, and greater attention paid to each animal's welfare."[79] And no doubt Niman's animals occasionally experience accidents or botched procedures that result in major and potentially irremediable suffering. In the book's narrative, Foer is struck by his sympathy and respect for Frank Niman, but out of concern for the animals, he still concludes it's better to avoid Niman Ranch products.[80]

I expect that for some readers, Foer's position will seem overly demanding. Perhaps Niman Ranch falls short of a standard whereby any serious discomfort imposed on animals is evidence of wrongdoing, but this seems like too stringent a benchmark to demand farmers meet. For one thing, as we discussed in Chapter 2, the animals at Niman Ranch wouldn't exist if not for the fact they're being raised for food. For another thing, these animals plausibly live far better lives than almost any animal in the wild. Perhaps we wouldn't want to say on such bases that Frank Niman may do whatever he likes to his animals—say, as long as their lives remain minimally worth living or better than what they'd experience in nature. But it arguably goes too far in the other direction to say it's wrong for Niman to run his farming operation unless he can guarantee his animals an existence in which nothing seriously unpleasant is ever done to them. After all, *people* don't live lives free from such impositions![81]

To assess the extent to which meat production counts as humane, we need standards that appropriately value farm animals' welfare without insisting nothing bad ever happens to them at farmers' hands. However, articulating such standards is easier said than done. If you're anything like me, you have only a modest understanding of the practical details of farming, and you're unlikely to be a reliable judge of the pros and cons of specific practices. Especially in cases where different considerations come into conflict—for example, when promoting an animal's physical health can be achieved most effectively through painful procedures or by obstructing natural behaviors[82]—it may be difficult to see what "humane treatment" would involve. The same is true in cases where the impacts of a particular practice depend not only on *what* is done but also on fine-grained details of *how* it's done.[83]

Complicating matters further, many of our potential sources of information have clear interests in driving us to certain conclusions. For example, we can predict that writers operating within the meat industry and mainstream veterinary profession will urge us to sympathize with farmers who follow standard industry practices. On the other hand, anti-meat activists will often be out to cast a negative light on these professionals and their behaviors. In this polarized environment, it can be difficult to remedy our ignorance without succumbing to bias, even if we try to achieve an "objective" outlook.

These challenges are made especially difficult by the fact that people can manipulate or distort our understanding without lying outright. It's often possible, for example, to make innocent things sound vile by describing them in terrible ways. Consider braces. Throughout the world, orthodontists force skin-tearing wires and obtrusive metal brackets into the mouths of young children, painfully wrenching their teeth into new positions for the sake of mere cosmetic appeal. The children are often forced to endure this torture for years at a time, experiencing gouged cheeks, sliced lips, and in some cases severe cavities and tooth decay around the bases of their brackets. Of course, most of us don't regard orthodontics as a great moral scandal, but it's nevertheless possible to make it sound like one without simply lying about it. For someone unfamiliar with braces, these hyperbolic descriptions might be difficult to refute, and it would certainly be possible for muckraking "investigators" to uncover ample evidence of each of these "horrors."[84]

On the other hand, it's equally possible to describe monstrous practices in ways that sound benign. For example, imagine a military sergeant is asked to investigate a possible terrorist plot. The sergeant responds by leading his squad to invade a town of innocent civilians, murdering those who get in their way and torturing the rest. Although the sergeant and his team nominally go through the motions of trying to extract information from the citizens, they're unsurprised when the search turns up nothing of substance, for they never expected to find anything in the first place. Clearly, these soldiers have behaved atrociously. But consider how the sergeant could describe what happened—even in great detail—without revealing any wrongdoing:

> In pursuing my mission, I ordered my troops to interview individuals with suspected terrorist ties, using enhanced interrogation techniques when deemed necessary to gain potentially life-saving information. Along the way, my team engaged and dispatched several hostile combatants, and some collateral damage was unfortunately incurred in the process. Sadly, in the end, we were forced to conclude our mission before any firm leads could be uncovered.

Such a summary would largely reflect the details of my original description of the scenario while obfuscating the awful nature of what happened.

The distorting power of language has analogs in other modes of information gathering as well. Just as it's possible to describe something in ways that sound terrible or benign, it's also often possible to capture photos and even videos that support vastly different moral assessments. Personal testimonialscan likewise be selected and manipulated to cast a favorable or unfavorable light—even when they avoid outright lies.

These reflections should make us wary of trusting our investigative capabilities when assessing meat industry participants' behavior. (Indeed, as you read this chapter, you should consider whether I've succeeded in providing a trustworthy overview!) On the one hand, we may worry about being blinded from the truth by farming interests trying to sugarcoat profit-driven misdeeds. On the other hand, we may worry about being whipped into a frenzy by animal rights activists who exaggerate how badly farm animals are treated.[85] Given our ignorance and vulnerability to manipulation, it seems reasonable to ask: are there experts out there who understand what's actually going on and can help clarify what standards are warranted?

In the arena of humane animal treatment, it turns out there are a number of organizations in the United States and abroad that have attempted to fill this role of expert evaluators. Some of the most prominent efforts have been undertaken by meat producers themselves in collaboration with veterinary professionals and government regulators. Others have arisen within the nonprofit sector to serve as independent sources of oversight. In the coming sections, we will examine these organizations' conclusions. Doing so will enable us to see that, even if we set our standards far lower than "perfection," we'll still have ample reason to reject the idea that the industry operates in an acceptably ethical way.

INDUSTRY STANDARDS

Every major meat-producing company insists it cares about its animals. Yet, as we've seen throughout this chapter, this hasn't stopped observers from raising wide-ranging criticisms against the industry's practices. As consumers and activists have directed greater scrutiny toward the industry, corporate leaders have worked with veterinarians and regulators to design explicit benchmarks by which all producers are judged. These benchmarks vary by species and market segment, but today there are National Chicken Council standards for chicken producers, Common Swine Industry Audits for pork producers, Beef Quality Assurance standards for beef producers, and North American Meat Institute standards for slaughterhouses.[86]

These standards cover many aspects of farming operations. For example, they require producers to publish standard operating procedures as well as plans for responding to the need to euthanize an animal or emergencies like power outages or natural disasters. All animal caretakers must receive annual training, and specialized tasks like vaccination, euthanasia, and catching and loading for transportation require additional training. Farm operations must be monitored regularly, and continuous records must be kept of animal health problems, medications, treatments, and mortalities. Indoor facilities need to be constructed from appropriate materials and provide adequate food, water, space, ventilation, and moisture control. There are guidelines for how farmers can catch, load, and transport animals and further guidelines for slaughterhouses to make sure animals are properly handled, stunned, and killed.

To supervise compliance with these standards, many companies—especially in the chicken and pork industries—undergo independent auditing by a group called PAACO, the Professional Animal Auditor Certification Organization. PAACO was formed in 2004 by a coalition of national veterinary and animal science organizations to enforce the new standards being formulated across the meat industry. Eight organizations are responsible for appointing PAACO's leadership: the American Associations of Avian Pathologists, Bovine Practitioners, and Swine Veterinarians; the American Dairy and Meat Science Associations; the American Registry of Professional Animal Scientists; the American Society of Animal Science; and the Poultry Science Association. In practice, these directors are drawn either from public universities or from companies within the meat industry itself.[87]

Although PAACO trains and certifies auditors, its function is mainly to enforce the meat industry's standards rather than criticize or change them. And even though the industry's benchmarks are set in collaboration with regulators and veterinary and animal science experts, it's hard to deny that meat producers play a prominent role in shaping the standards used to judge their operations. These facts about how most meat producers are audited raise obvious questions. Do PAACO's audits actually confirm that animal welfare is being protected? Do the industry's standards touch on all the most important criteria for animals' wellbeing? Do they set suitably ambitious requirements? Do they take a sufficiently strict stance against practices that benefit companies at animals' expense? Or has the meat industry simply defined "humane" treatment in terms of whatever its members consider appropriate behavior?

Skepticism toward the industry's self-monitoring is exacerbated by the fact that PAACO's auditing procedures leave considerable room for facilities to score low on specific benchmarks without being declared as "failing." For example, PAACO evaluates many poultry operations using the National Chicken Council Animal Welfare Audit Checklist.[88] This checklist awards a maximum of 1,730 points across a variety of categories, but only 1,510 points are needed to pass (about 87%).[89] Because of this leeway, it would be possible for a company to pass its audit even if, for example, it had taken no corrective action in response to reported equipment injuries to chicks (a 20-point deduction),[90] its vehicles for transporting chicks lacked adequate temperature control capabilities (a 10-point deduction),[91] its growing houses were filled with caked and wet litter (a 40-point deduction),[92] one in every dozen chicks proved unable to walk after gentle encouragement (a 20-point deduction),[93] more than 10% of birds' feet displayed sores or scabs covering more than half the footpad (a 20-point deduction),[94] one in every 25 birds had experienced a broken or dislocated wing prior to stunning (a 20-point deduction),[95] and one in every 50 chickens passed through the stunner without being rendered unconscious (a 20-point deduction).[96]

As this illustration shows, companies can fall significantly short of the National Chicken Council's standards without failing their PAACO audits. But in some parts of the meat industry, PAACO is not even asked to "pass" or "fail" farming operations in the first place. For example, the Common Swine Industry Audit categorically prohibits pork producers from willful abuse, neglect, and inhumane euthanasia,[97] but beyond this, it doesn't specify a minimum overall level of performance needed to "pass" the assessment. Instead, it simply scores each facility's performance in a way that enables comparison with others in the industry. Thus, instead of defining a benchmark for what counts as acceptable, the Common Swine Industry Audit relies on packers and other market actors to enforce their own standards for what they consider appropriate relative to its scoring system.[98]

These considerations help us see that although the meat industry's self-imposed standards undoubtedly provide a key line of defense against mistreatment and abuse, they exhibit important and obvious weaknesses as a mechanism for addressing concerns about the industry's practices. Even if we were willing to grant that the industry has identified reasonable standards for what counts as humane treatment of animals, the refusal to enforce those standards strictly would be cause for concern. But it's also unclear whether we should grant the legitimacy of the industry's standards in the first place. At the very least, it seems reasonable to seek another source of insight into what standards are appropriate for judging the industry's operations.

INDEPENDENT CERTIFICATIONS

Several nonprofits have augmented the meat industry's standards by establishing their own benchmarks for humane animal treatment. These organizations include American Humane, Humane Farm Animal Care, A Greener World, and Global Animal Partnership. In many respects, these groups' standards align with those set by the industry. For example, all agree that rigorous planning and information gathering are at the heart of humane animal treatment. Each requires the farms they certify to have comprehensive plans for animal health, nutrition, and emergencies (particularly those that might cut off water or electricity). Each requires producers to keep extensive records of their procedures and animals' performance. Each requires remedial action when negative outcomes begin to arise. And each requires proper training for all workers who interact with animals.

In contrast to the industry's standards, however, these organizations identify certain common practices that must be avoided for an operation to be certified as "humane." To cite just one illustration, pork producers sometimes desire to discourage pigs from using their snouts to root in the ground (for example, to prevent them from doing damage to pasture land). One way to achieve this is by fitting pigs with a nose piercing in the form of a ring. The ring makes it uncomfortable for pigs to root, thus addressing the rooting "problem," and the Common Swine Industry Audit singles out nose ringing as the only acceptable reason for intentionally causing physical damage to a pig's snout.[99] However, since pigs' snouts are incredibly sensitive parts of their body, the rings can also be a significant and chronic source of pain. Moreover, rooting is one of the main ways pigs are naturally disposed to spend their time,[100] so preventing it imposes a major restriction to their ability to exhibit their species' characteristic behaviors. For these reasons, every independent certifying organization prohibits nose ringing as inhumane.[101]

Nose ringing provides an example of a common practice independent certifiers reject outright. Yet, there are also cases where these organizations grant that certain common practices *can* be acceptable while imposing stricter standards for *how* they may be performed than the industry sets for itself. For example, when chickens are caught for transport, it's typical for workers to carry multiple birds to minimize the number of trips they must take to and from the transport modules. This is usually accomplished by holding chickens upside down by the legs. National Chicken Council guidelines indicate that in chicken houses with a target weight of over 5 lbs per chicken, workers may carry up to five birds per hand during catching. (Smaller chickens may be carried ten per hand.[102]) But independent certifiers broadly agree that carrying this many birds at once creates too much risk to animals, mandating lower limits for the farms they certify.[103]

The wide agreement on certain standards among independent animal welfare organizations provides good evidence they track genuine requirements for humane treatment—requirements that don't always align with the standards the industry imposes on itself. Things get more difficult, however, when it comes to areas where the nonprofits disagree among themselves. Consider, for example, the question of whether humanely raised chickens and pigs need access to outdoor spaces or whether it's OK to raise them completely indoors. A 2016 survey by Consumer Reports saw 78% of consumers opine that animal products should only be labeled as "humanely raised" if the animals in question lived at least part of their lives outside.[104] Perhaps surprisingly, however, independent animal welfare evaluators are divided on whether this should be a requirement. Two of the most prominent welfare labeling organizations, American Humane and Humane Farm Animal Care, don't require producers to provide chickens or pigs with outdoor access, insisting it's possible for all-indoor operations to qualify as humane.[105] A Greener World disagrees, requiring for its labels that all animals have ready access to outdoor spaces and even imposing stringent guidelines for how these spaces may be laid out.[106] Complicating matters further, Global Animal Partnership offers multiple levels (which it calls "Steps") for its Animal Welfare Certified labels, allowing consumers to decide what standards they personally consider appropriate: Steps 1 and 2 allow all-indoor production; Steps 3 and above do not.[107]

Disagreements among independent evaluators arise in more granular forms as well. For example, as we saw earlier in this chapter, it's a common practice among chicken farmers to expose broilers to artificial light since this encourages them to eat more and grow faster. Increased growth rates can mean higher profits for growers, but these can come at potentially high costs to animals' welfare since chickens can be susceptible to serious health problems if they grow too fast. Ensuring all chickens get adequate time in the dark is thus a commonsense requirement for humane production. But how much is needed? Answers vary widely. The National Chicken Council requires at least four hours of darkness per day, which may be divided into increments of one, two, or four hours.[108] American Humane is a bit stricter, insisting on four *continuous* hours of darkness per day (unless natural sunlight makes this impossible).[109] Humane Farm Animal Care goes further, demanding six continuous hours per day,[110] and

A Greener World goes further still, demanding eight continuous hours.[111] (Once again, Global Animal Partnership offers multiple levels, requiring six hours for Steps 1–2 and eight hours for Steps 3 and above.[112])

Along similar lines, when chickens are brought from their growing farms to the plants where they're slaughtered, they are cut off from food while they're caught, transported, and processed. Obviously, depriving a chicken of food for too long is inhumane. But how long is "too long?" The National Chicken Council sets the maximum allowable time without food at 18 hours[113]; American Humane sets it at 16 hours[114]; Global Animal Partnership and Humane Farm Animal Care say 12 hours[115]; and A Greener World says 8 hours except when birds are caught at night and slaughtered in the morning.[116]

Independent animal welfare certifications thus reflect wide-ranging levels of stringency in what is considered acceptably "humane." Unsurprisingly, these differing standards often track underlying differences in the companies with which the labeling organizations work. For example, A Greener World claims its strict standards "have been proven to be achievable by the vast majority of farm situations."[117] However, in practice, the organization focuses primarily on small-scale producers who serve customers willing to pay premium prices at farmers' markets or farm-to-table restaurants.[118] On the other end of the spectrum, American Humane works with some of the largest meat producers in the United States. Its American Humane Certified label appears on mainstream supermarket brands such as Butterball, Case Farms Chicken, and Foster Farms.[119] The Certified Humane label from Humane Farm Animal Care occupies a sort of middle ground, both in terms of demandingness and the kinds of companies it certifies.[120] And with its multiple "Steps," the Animal Welfare Certified program by Global Animal Partnership targets companies spanning the full industry spectrum.[121]

These differing relationships between independent evaluators and the meat industry present us with challenging questions about which assessments to consider most reliable when deciding what "humane" treatment actually requires. On the one hand, we might worry that certain organizations have adopted lower than fully humane standards in an effort to attract large corporate producers to participate. In such cases, we may sympathize with the certifiers' desire to affect as many animals as possible. Still, we may wonder whether earning that certifier's label truly means a company has operated humanely. On the other hand, we may worry that other organizations are overly beholden to activists, ideologues, and persnickety consumers, adopting standards that reflect not so much what morality requires as what will assure the most demanding judges that animals are receiving the best care possible.

In this book, I don't want to try to settle on the best specific standards for assessing when animals are being treated humanely. Instead, I'll settle for three main observations. First, independent nonprofit evaluators have converged on more stringent animal welfare standards than the industry imposes on itself—not along every dimension, but among many. This doesn't necessarily prove the industry's standards are too lax since it would hardly make sense for organizations to bother designing and promulgating separate benchmarks if they didn't go beyond prevailing industry norms. But insofar as independent evaluators agree many mainstream practices should be eliminated and others need adjusting, this provides at least some reason to believe these areas of incongruence represent genuine problems for the animals we eat.

Second, in marked contrast to the practices of organizations like PAACO, independent animal welfare certifiers tend to enforce their standards strictly. Generally, a producer seeking certification from one of these nonprofits needs to meet *all* relevant standards (or petition for a special exemption from a particular rule). Simply meeting *most* of the standards is typically not enough to be certified as "humane." (The major exception here is the American Humane Certified label. Although American Humane requires 100% compliance for broiler chicken operations,[122] pork and beef producers can receive the label as long as they earn over 85% of the points available on the organization's audit.[123])

Finally, even if we accept the most lenient of the independent nonprofits' standards as reflecting the true requirements for humane treatment, we'll find that the vast majority of large industry players don't make the grade—or at least not in a way we can verify from the outside. The top producer in the chicken industry (Tyson Foods) raised and slaughtered nearly 2 billion chickens in 2020. The second-largest producer (Pilgrim's Pride) added nearly 1.6 billion more. The companies rounding out the top five (Koch Foods, Sanderson Farms, and Perdue Foods) contributed close to another 2 billion chickens.[124] Of these companies, only Perdue certifies any of its chicken operations with any organization besides PAACO. (Perdue works with Global Animal Partnership to certify its organic chickens at levels ranging from Steps 2 to 4, and it hires PAACO to implement standards for the rest of its operations that are more stringent than those developed by the National Chicken Council.[125])

Along similar lines, Smithfield Foods, the unquestioned leader of the US pork industry, is uncertified by any independent nonprofit. In the beef industry, market-leading Tyson runs a subsidiary, Open Prairie Natural Meats, which has achieved Step 1 certification with Global Animal Partnership.[126] But the vast majority of their beef operations are monitored only by industry-affiliated auditors, and the same is true for other powers like Cargill, JBS, and National Beef.

Together, these reflections make it reasonable to conclude that virtually all the meat we encounter on supermarket shelves and restaurant menus has been produced in ways we cannot verify as humane. Moreover, this is true even if we're willing to defer to the most permissive standards from independent nonprofit certifiers. The meat industry's self-imposed standards are plausibly not stringent enough to capture what animals truly deserve, and they are also not strictly enforced. Thus, we have little reason to believe the animals we eat receive adequate treatment from the companies that raise them. In an industry that raised 35.1 million cows, 139.4 million pigs, and 9.25 billion broiler chickens in 2020 in the United States alone,[127] these shortcomings represent an ethical problem of truly gargantuan proportions.

THE PROBLEMS ARE REAL

Like all too many of the products we consume, meat is linked to numerous ills: harsh conditions for workers, negative impacts on the environment, and threats to public health. But the meat industry stands apart from other sources of problems in virtue of the great burdens it imposes on animals in the absence of adequate safeguards to protect them. Even by relatively permissive standards of what counts as "humane," none of the largest meat producers in the United States can provide reasonable assurance their operations make the grade. Considering these shortfalls alongside the litany of other complaints about equity, sustainability, and public health, it seems fair to conclude something is seriously wrong with how meat is actually produced.

In the previous chapter, I argued that if meat were produced humanely, equitably, sustainably, and safely, eating it would be OK. But what about meat that's not produced that way? Is it OK to eat meat linked to such serious concerns about animals, workers, the environment, and public health? This is the question I'll tackle in the chapters to come.

I have argued that if every animal were raised humanely, equitably, sustainably, and safely, eating meat would plausibly be OK. However, as we saw in the previous chapter, most meat is not produced so scrupulously. The vast majority of what's available in supermarkets and restaurants is linked to serious ethical concerns about animals, workers, the environment, and public health. Many vegetarians think these problems give us clear moral marching orders: until the industry gets its act together, we should avoid consuming its products. Even if it might be possible in principle to be a conscientious omnivore, these vegetarians claim it's wrong to eat meat in practice, given how it's almost always produced.

My aim over the next three chapters will be to show why this view is mistaken. Although many serious problems can be traced to the meat industry, this doesn't mean it's wrong to eat meat—even meat produced in the problematic ways we've discussed. To defend this view, I'll need to address a variety of arguments for responding to the meat industry's problems by becoming vegetarian. Some of these arguments focus on the impacts of our dietary choices on the meat industry's behavior. Others emphasize the significance of abstaining from actions we wish no one would take. Others still revolve around the ways meat-eaters position themselves relative to

DOI: 10.4324/9781003221944-4

the meat industry's wrongs. Since it would be a mistake to try to refute all these diverging arguments at once, I'll examine each type in turn over the chapters to come.

The arguments I'll examine in this chapter begin from the idea that when people eat meat, they exacerbate the problems we've discussed—animal mistreatment, worker exploitation, environmental degradation, and public health endangerment. On the other hand, when people *stop* eating meat, they're held to contribute to alleviating these problems. Since the problems are so serious and since it would be good if they went away, we're invited to conclude that it's wrong to eat meat and obligatory to become vegetarians instead.

This chapter argues that this general strategy for vindicating vegetarianism fails. As long as the case for vegetarianism revolves around its causal impacts in preventing bad things from happening, we won't find a specific moral duty to abstain from meat. Since there are other arguments for vegetarianism, rejecting this one line of reasoning won't directly prove it's OK to eat meat. However, this chapter will show that a particularly intuitive and popular style of vegetarian argument is unpersuasive, and so vegetarians need a different strategy if they hope to vindicate their view.[1]

WHAT HAPPENS WHEN A PERSON EATS MEAT?

The meat industry doesn't operate just for fun: to the extent that it mistreats animals, exploits workers, degrades the environment, and endangers public health, it does these things to make money. Further, the reason it *can* make money from its objectionable activities is that meat-eaters purchase its products. If people stopped buying meat, the industry would cease to exist. So, it seems natural to infer that when someone eats meat, they cause animals to suffer, workers to be exploited, the environment to deteriorate, and public health to be put at risk. They cause all these bad things to happen, and in all likelihood, they have no compelling excuse. (Recall our discussion in Chapter 1 of some potential excuses, none of which were convincing.) If all this is true, then it might seem to add up to a clear case for avoiding meat. Insofar as meat-eating causes terrible things to happen without any persuasive justification, it seems clear consumers should abstain.

However, difficulties begin to appear for this argument when one tries to clarify which terrible things the individual meat-eater causes to happen. Intuitively, it might seem sensible to say that when someone eats a piece of meat, they're responsible for causing whatever problems resulted from its production. For instance, suppose I buy a package of pork chops at the supermarket. The pork chops came from a pig that was raised in harsh conditions. The pig was handled by workers who were treated badly by their employers. This same company was fouling the air and water with pollution and endangering public health with its imperfect biosecurity protocols. By eating my pork chop, one might think, I've caused these bad things to happen. (Or, at any rate, I've caused some portion of them. Many other consumers presumably share the responsibility since the mistreated pig, exploited workers, environmental impacts, and public health threats generated far more than just my pork chops. For the sake of focusing on other more important issues, though, we can set aside the matter of how to divide the responsibility among each consumer as a kind of accounting question that's unlikely to alter the moral bottom line.)

This depiction of the causal relationship between the individual meat-eater's purchase and the industry's actions is straightforward enough. However, it has a shortcoming: it gets the sequence of events backward. The suffering of the pig, exploitation of the workers, polluting of the environment, and endangerment of public health all took place considerably before I bought my pork chops. The corporate plans that put these problems into motion were adopted even earlier. Moreover, these things happened without any input from me. The pork chops were not "made to order" at my request: the company that produced them did so on the basis of highly general projections of what market conditions would be like in future months and years.[2] By the time I bought my pork chops, my opportunity to influence any of these decisions had long since passed. The mistreated pig, exploited workers, polluted environment, and public health risks were obviously connected to my eventual decision to eat pork chops (a point we'll discuss in more depth in Chapter 6). But given the timeline according to which these events took place, it would be a mistake to say the latter *caused* the former to happen. If we can properly describe my decision to eat pork chops as *causing* something to happen, it needs to be something that happens *after* I get involved in the picture. That can't be the animal mistreatment, worker exploitation, environmental degradation, or public health endangerment that went into my pork chop. Those things all happened before I intervened.

Yet, there may seem to be an easy way to fix the error. Perhaps we could say that when I buy and eat my pork chops, I cause the meat industry to produce more in the future than would otherwise have been the case. In other words, perhaps the bad things I cause are not the problems that arose in producing my pork chops; rather, they're the problems that result from the increased production later on.

For this reformulated argument to work, it would need to be the case that buying pork chops today will typically result in additional pork chops (or other meat products) eventually being produced. If my decision to eat pork chops predictably had no such impact on the meat industry's future actions—that is, if the industry would likely produce the same amount of meat regardless of my decision—then the argument would fail. My decision to eat meat would have no causal impact on the problems produced by the industry's behavior.

The question thus becomes whether we should expect an individual's decision to consume a piece of meat to result in the production of additional meat in the future. In what follows, I'll argue the answer is no. When a person buys and consumes meat at typical supermarkets and restaurants, they're highly unlikely to cause meat companies to mistreat more animals, exploit more workers, produce more environmental impacts, or create greater public health risks. What any individual consumer causes the industry to do (or not do) through their dietary decisions is *nothing*. We may refer to this claim that individual meat-eaters have no impact on the meat industry's behavior as the Inefficacy Thesis (i.e., the thesis that individual meat-eaters are *inefficacious*—they have no effect).[3]

On the face of it, this Inefficacy Thesis may seem absurd. Just a few pages ago, I said the meat industry does what it does because meat-eaters pay for its products. So, how could it be true that when individuals purchase meat to consume, they don't cause the industry to produce additional meat? In building toward an answer, it'll be useful to begin by illustrating how it's *possible* for things like this to happen.

HOW INEFFICACY IS POSSIBLE

Imagine I'm a football fan with tickets to see my local team play. Unfortunately, I'm sensitive to noise, and I can't bear to sit for hours with people screaming into my unprotected ears. I'm therefore planning to bring noise protection when I go to the game. However, blocking out *too much* noise would deprive me of the true gameday experience. So, I've decided to watch some of the team's earlier games on TV to assess how loud the stadium actually gets, aiming to select some earplugs or earmuffs that are well suited to that level of noise. Happily, for my purposes, I know the stadium periodically displays a decibel meter on the jumbotron to measure the noise level of the crowd. (To my chagrin, the reason for doing this is to encourage fans to scream even more loudly—but let's set that aside.) I know from personal experience this meter is accurate. I've therefore set up my television with a decibel meter, and it's calibrated so I know exactly how the decibels measured in the stadium equate to those measured in my house. With these preparations complete, I begin my investigation into how best to protect myself from the stadium's unbearable noise.

Now, imagine you're a fan attending a football game I'm watching. When you cheer, you contribute to the noise level in the stadium, which gets captured by the broadcasters' microphones, transmitted to my television, measured by my decibel meter, and ultimately interpreted by me. Clearly, the actions of stadium-goers like you will determine which earplugs or earmuffs I bring to the game. But does this mean that, by screaming or refraining from screaming, you can alter my plans?

Plausibly, the answer is no. For one thing, there are many ways in which the effects of your decision might get swallowed up before I have an opportunity to perceive them. The microphones in the stadium might not be sensitive enough to register a difference in sound levels from a single fan's screaming. Even if they did register such a difference, the TV station might not broadcast in high enough fidelity to transmit the information to my house. Even if the information did arrive at my television, my speakers might not be constructed well enough to reproduce such a subtle difference in sound. And even if the speakers produced a different sound, my decibel meter might not be sensitive enough to display the change.

Further, even if my decibel meter did manage to register the fact that you had altered the noise level in the stadium, this might still have no impact on my decision. In all likelihood, I won't base my choice of which earplugs or earmuffs to bring to the game on tiny momentary fluctuations in the stadium's noise level. Instead, I'll base my decision on the general range of noise levels over a typical game. Indeed, it would seem silly for me to choose a particular form of noise protection if the appropriateness of that choice hung on whether a particular fan on gameday decided to scream or not. A smarter decision would be to select an option that would deliver satisfactory results regardless of what any single fan in the stadium chose to do.

In this example, then, two things are true at the same time. First, my decision about what noise protection to bring to the game depends on the screaming in the stadium. (If everyone stopped screaming, I wouldn't need protection, and the type of protection I bring depends on the general level of noise people make.) But second, it doesn't follow automatically from this that any individual fan has the power to alter my behavior by changing how much—or whether—they scream. In fact, in this particular example, it's not just possible for a fan to have zero impact on my decision: it's virtually guaranteed. Given the multi-layered opportunities for a single fan to fail to affect my decision, an Inefficacy Thesis would seem highly plausible in the context of this case.

Thinking through this illustration hopefully helps clarify why it's not absurd to think an Inefficacy Thesis could apply in the context of meat-eating. But it remains to be shown that similar factors *actually do* operate in the market for meat. To establish this latter claim, let's work back through the structure of the stadium example to show the same basic points apply to meat-eating. The stadium case involved two main stages at which a fan's behavior could be rendered inefficacious. First, on the way from the stadium to my home, the signal communicating the fan's behavior could be lost, whether because it wasn't picked up by the microphone, broadcast to the television, reproduced by the TV speakers, or captured by the decibel meter. Second, even if the information about the fan's behavior were registered, it could still fail to change the decision. For better or worse, both kinds of obstacles exist in the market for meat.

TRANSMISSION UP THE SUPPLY CHAIN

Why might a consumer's decision about whether to eat meat fail to be apprehended by producers? For illustration, suppose once again I'm deciding whether to buy a pack of pork chops. If I do this, it'll mean the pack of pork chops gets sold by the supermarket, whereas if I opt for tofu stir-fry instead, my pork chops will remain on the shelf. Intuitively, we might expect the difference between these two outcomes to be reflected in how the supermarket stocks its shelves, resulting in more pork chops ordered in the former scenario than the latter and hence more pork chops ultimately demanded from producers.

In practice, however, this is far from guaranteed. One reason for this is that grocers expect demand for any particular product to fluctuate.[4] Since most people don't eat the same things every week, the precise set of products they'll buy in a trip to the grocery store will vary. Moreover, customers themselves come and go: a person who shops at one store this week may take their business elsewhere next week, only to return a week later. A grocer's job is not to predict consumers' behavior at this level of detail. Rather, their task is to zoom out to the level of statistical regularities and ask what products must generally be in stock and in what quantities so customers are sufficiently satisfied and profits keep rolling in.

These decisions require grocers to balance two competing considerations. On the one hand, products like fresh meat cost money, and they tend to spoil quickly. A supermarket that stocks more meat than consumers will buy loses money from the waste. On the other hand, running out of products is also costly. If a customer arrives to buy pork chops and none are available—or the selection is underwhelming—that might mean a lost sale and lower profits (unless the customer buys something else instead). Moreover, customers who can't predictably get the products they want may decide to shop at a different store in the future. There is thus something to gain from having extra products on hand to prevent the possibility of displeasing customers, even if this will often result in some spoiling before they're sold. In practice, grocers typically resolve this balancing act in favor of having some amount of "expected waste." In the United States, as much as 5% of all meat acquired by supermarkets is ultimately thrown away.[5]

Although supermarkets expect to waste some proportion of the meat they buy, they also have many options for dealing with slow-selling meat besides allowing it to spoil. For example, a grocer who sees a pack of pork chops nearing expiration can place a "sale" or "clearance" sticker on it to entice customers with a discount. These might be people who would otherwise have bought fresher cuts of meat, or they could be people who would have bought no meat at all if not for the special offer. For items that are really selling slowly, grocers can run a sale or special and advertise it in their weekly circular ad. Alternatively, grocers can cook the meat to sell from the prepared food case. (This is how many rotisserie chickens, barbecue rib dinners, and beef and barley soups come into existence.) One way or another, a smart grocer will minimize the number of products that rot on their shelves by taking extra steps to encourage customers to buy them. And when this fails—as it often does—they'll simply discard the spoiled products and move on.[6]

Grocers expect fluctuations in demand. They have incentives to overstock. They have contingency options for dealing with unsold meat. And they expect to discard some portion of their products as a matter of course. For all these reasons, supermarkets represent an important stage at which a consumer's decision whether to buy meat can fail to be transmitted further up the supply chain. One customer's decision to choose pork chops over tofu stir-fry or stir-fry over pork chops are both fully consistent with what a grocer expects on a given afternoon. Hence, the grocer may continue placing meat orders in the same way regardless of what the customer chooses. When this happens, the consumer's decision of what to eat is rendered inefficacious. Because it fails to be transmitted up the supply chain to producers, it has no hope of changing how those producers conduct their operations.[7]

We can say much the same thing about ordering meat in restaurants. Typically, when a restaurant orders a certain amount of meat for the week, it faces the same basic prospect of fluctuating demand for individual menu items and must strike the same basic balance between wasting ingredients and running out of them. Restaurants finding themselves with excess ingredients also often accelerate their sale—for example, in the form of a "daily special" or "soup of the day." As a last resort, restaurants will discard what they cannot use, treating this as simply one of the costs of doing business in their predictably unpredictable industry.

We can further compound these points by noticing that even supermarkets and restaurants don't necessarily order their meat directly from the companies that produce it. Many work instead with third-party meat distributors who act as intermediaries between producers and retailers. Like supermarkets and restaurants, these distributors also operate in fluctuating markets, and they too have options for accelerating the sale of products that happen not to be moving. So, even if a consumer *does* cause a supermarket or restaurant to change the amount of meat it orders, this change might still get swallowed up before it reaches the top of the supply chain.

Taking things one final step further, even when information about changes in consumer behavior does reach the top of the supply chain, there's still a considerable likelihood the information will fail to be perceived by anyone who actually makes decisions. Although it's technically true the difference would be recorded somewhere in some company's sales data, firms with annual revenues in the billions of dollars don't concern their human decision makers with information at the level of individual consumer purchases. They record figures in millions of dollars, millions of hogs, millions of pounds, and so on. In all likelihood, the change in a company's performance figures produced by a small change to a single supermarket or restaurant order would be rounded off by a computer before any corporate employee laid eyes on it.

RESPONSIVENESS TO CHANGES

There are strong reasons to doubt that when a single consumer chooses to buy (or not buy) a particular piece of meat, information about this choice will be transmitted up the supply chain to meat industry decision makers. Still, it's not *impossible* for this to occur. In rare cases, a person's decision to have tofu stir-fry instead of pork chops could lead to a smaller order being made from a company like Smithfield Foods and to this change being presented to Smithfield decision makers in the form of a small change in sales numbers. To take an especially optimistic example: the change could push a particular figure over a rounding threshold, such that total sales of fresh pork might be reported as $5,397.3 million instead of $5,397.4 million, or average hog sale prices reported as $61.47 per 100 lbs instead of $61.48 per $100 lbs. Even if this happened, however, it still wouldn't guarantee an impact on the meat producer's operations. In fact, the most likely outcome remains that the producer would do nothing differently as a result of the change.[8]

To begin to see why, consider that meat producers also operate in markets where changing conditions are commonplace. Over a given year, demand will fluctuate for each product a company sells, and so will the prices charged by other firms for similar products. To stay competitive, companies need to be proactive in adjusting prices and monitoring inventories. Like supermarkets and restaurants, they can respond to slow sales through advertising, specials, coupons, and even shifting products across segments so that (for instance) poorly selling cuts of fresh meat are repurposed as prepared foods. The need for measures like these is not a deviation from these companies' ordinary course of business: rather, it's an expected part of their regular operations.

On the other side of the ledger, meat companies also face significant variability in their farms' operations. Animal health and performance can never be completely guaranteed: as we saw in the previous chapter, every farm expects to suffer some degree of loss and poor outcomes, with some cohorts enduring greater hardships than others. Farmers also rely on a variety of inputs that themselves vary in price and quality.[9] For instance, animal feed represents one of the biggest costs faced by growers, and feed prices can fluctuate substantially over a given year. Companies can take adaptive action to reduce the impacts of these changes: for example, if soybean prices rise, there may be some options for shifting pigs to a diet richer in some other food, such as corn. But producers must ultimately be prepared for variability in their feed costs that they can't completely avoid. We can say similar things about labor costs, unplanned maintenance, prices of water, electricity, and fuel, and so on. Even changes in the weather can affect a given farm's performance.

Taken together, these facts about the meat industry's operating environment suggest the task of aligning production decisions to sales expectations is necessarily imprecise. Certainly, companies articulate plans to raise particular numbers of animals at particular facilities to produce particular amounts of meat at particular costs. Likewise, they aim to sell particular quantities of particular products across particular segments for particular prices. But even as these plans are being made, they're not construed as precise projections of how things will go. Rather, they represent general targets, developed with the recognition that changing circumstances along a wide range of dimensions will affect what actually happens in a given year.[10]

Given this, how likely is it that a single supermarket or restaurant ordering less of a particular product on a particular occasion will affect a company's future operations? In virtually every case, it seems clear the answer will be: not at all. Rather than adjusting to such a minuscule difference in the outcomes of their operations, companies will almost certainly forge ahead just as they would have if the relevant purchase had occurred in full. This result is made especially likely by the fact that, as we've already seen, these companies' decisions have to do with *future* output. Although weak sales in the present may to revised expectations for how things will go down the road, it's hard to imagine a company substantially revising its long-term projections in response to a tiny change in sales data caused by a single customer's purchase. This is not to say it *couldn't* happen, of course. However, the chances are reasonably described as so small as to be practically insignificant.[11]

We can now see why the situation faced by consumers in the market for meat is analogous to what we saw in the stadium example above. In that illustration, my choice of noise protection depended on how loud I expected the stadium to be, and those expectations were sensitive to the stadium's loudness during prior games. However, it didn't follow that any individual fan had the power to alter my actions by screaming or remaining silent. For one thing, the signal from any single fan's behavior could be swallowed up before making it to me. But even if it didn't get swallowed up, I would probably take the same course of action regardless of how any single fan behaved.

We find similar dynamics in markets for meat. Although producers' decisions are based on demand for their products, it doesn't follow that any single consumer has the power to affect what these producers do. In all likelihood, information about an individual's purchase will never make it all the way up the supply chain for producers to consider. And even if it did, producers would likely make the same decisions about future production regardless. Thus, when it comes to individuals' choices of whether to eat meat, an Inefficacy Thesis seems well supported. Even though the meat industry is connected to many serious problems, and even though its behavior is driven by consumer demand, the marginal impact of any individual meat-eater on the industry's behavior is *nothing*.

PARTICIPATING IN A MOVEMENT

If every time you ate a piece of chicken, pork, or beef, you caused animals to suffer, workers to be exploited, the environment to deteriorate, and public health to be endangered, the case against meat-eating would be powerful. As we've seen, however, this is not how things work: what you put in your mouth is unlikely to affect the meat industry's problems. Still, it would be hasty to conclude on this basis that eating meat is OK, for there are still a variety of ways to defend vegetarianism even if each individual's actions fail to alter the meat industry's behavior.

One such argument observes that, even if one person can't influence the meat industry by changing their diet, millions of people acting in concert most certainly can—and in fact, they do so in practice.[12] Over the past 50 years, millions of people worldwide have given up meat in response to the industry's bad behavior. In truth, as I've said before in this book, the vast majority of people who do this remain vegetarians only temporarily. (Of Americans who report having practiced vegetarianism at one time, over 80% report having gone back to eating meat.[13]) But even these temporary vegetarians help make it so, at any given moment, a substantial subset of the population refuses to buy meat from mainstream producers.

There's no denying that the vegetarian movement as a whole has had major impacts on the meat industry. For one thing, the movement's efforts make it so less meat is produced than there would otherwise be. But vegetarians have also successfully pushed for important reforms in how meat is produced through political lobbying and mobilizing public opinion with protests and exposés. Vegetarians have raised awareness of the worst aspects of mainstream meat production, and even many meat-eaters have responded by consuming less meat, targeting products with "humane" labels, and integrating more plant-based foods into their diets. The prospect of selling to vegetarians has also facilitated the emergence of numerous non-meat food offerings, from vegetarian dishes at restaurants to "meat alternatives" in grocery stores. All these developments can be ascribed largely to people deciding to act against the meat industry's behavior by becoming vegetarians. (Even this book wouldn't exist if not for them.)

Notice these *collective* impacts can exist without it being true that any vegetarian produces an impact *individually*. We can see this by looking back at the stadium example. It seems clear that if a few thousand fans decided to keep silent together, this might make a significant difference to the overall noise level, even if none of them could make a noticeable impact on their own by changing whether or not they screamed. In the same way, even if the Inefficacy Thesis is true at the level of each individual meat-eater, large numbers of consumers acting together can still make a significant difference.[14]

This ability of vegetarians to collectively influence the meat industry's behavior seems like a reason to avoid eating meat. Insofar as the vegetarian movement has a significant positive impact on the problems of animal suffering, worker exploitation, environmental degradation, and public health endangerment—and insofar as those impacts depend on contributions from individuals—there's clearly something valuable about people's decisions to give up meat and become vegetarians. Again, this value doesn't come from the marginal impact of any single vegetarian's contribution (which we have good reason to think is insignificant). Rather, it comes from the fact that each vegetarian is doing their part to create a collective impact that's significant when taken as a whole.[15]

As far as it goes, this line of reasoning is correct: there is something good about contributing to vegetarianism's positive impacts. However, this doesn't directly show that eating meat is wrong. To see why, consider that vegetarianism is just one of many ways people can (and do) come together to act on the world's ills. For example, those who defend international human rights, relieve global poverty, or conduct medical research contribute to crucial progress on serious problems. The same is true of those who take to the streets against ongoing injustice, political corruption, and the neglect of community needs. Opportunities for action surround us: we can volunteer to tutor local schoolchildren, collect cans for the food bank, write letters to our political representatives, and on and on. We can say of all these enterprises that there's something valuable about contributing to them, and hence we have at least some reason to do so. But it doesn't follow that for any given one of these causes, contributing is morally obligatory. In a world full of serious problems, it's plausible that each of us has a duty to act, but no one is obligated to promote every worthy cause in every possible way. It seems entirely possible to live an ethical life while taking no significant action to support many important causes.

If this is true, then vegetarians can't rest their case on simply claiming their cause is a good one that relies on individual contributions to succeed. For we could say this same thing on behalf of countless movements combating countless problems around the world. What vegetarians need to show is that their specific form of activism is more than just one option among a wide range of alternatives. They need to show there's something special about vegetarianism that gives it more of a claim to people's participation than the many other movements that could use additional help.

We can make the issue clearer by considering an analogy. Imagine you're out doing errands with your small child, and things are taking longer than you anticipated. Your child is hungry and eventually begins to cry. A restaurateur sees your predicament and invites you to dine in their establishment. As a parent, you're presumably morally required to ensure your child is fed. Insofar as the restaurateur can provide you with food, it would seem accurate to say you have at least some reason to go to their restaurant, and there would be something valuable about doing so. Even so, it seems clear you're not *specifically required* to dine in this particular restaurant since there are other ways for you to satisfy your obligation as well. For example, you could rush your child home, pop over to a nearby supermarket, or choose to go to a different restaurant. For all we know, you might even have packed a snack for just this kind of situation. Eating at this restaurant is *one way* for you to satisfy your obligation to your child, but it's just one option among many. Because of this, it's entirely possible for you to decline this offer without doing anything wrong.

In much the same way, even if we grant people have a duty to help tackle our world's serious problems, we may nevertheless suspect that vegetarianism is just one option among many for satisfying this duty. If the argument for vegetarianism is simply that vegetarians mitigate important harms, then this puts vegetarian activists in a similar position as the restaurateur. As in the restaurant story, there is an obligation we can satisfy by joining the vegetarian movement (i.e., the obligation to contribute to combating the world's problems). However, there also seem to be many other options for fulfilling that duty. We could, for example, decide to focus instead on fighting racial oppression, civil rights abuses, species extinctions, or any of a host of other problems. At least on this way of setting up the dialectic, it would appear a person could decline to become a vegetarian without necessarily doing anything wrong.

Plainly, ethical vegetarians don't accept this way of characterizing the case for avoiding meat. They don't see vegetarianism as just one option among many for fulfilling one's moral duties; rather, they regard meat-eating as something *everyone* should avoid. But we should ask: why would this be so? What makes vegetarianism specifically required of us instead of just one of many ways we can contribute to an important cause?

WHY CHOOSE?

The line of reasoning presented above casts vegetarianism as just one of many ways we can act on the world's problems. Yet, this way of framing the issue suggests we must *choose* between avoiding meat and pursuing other forms of activism. One way to defend the claim it's wrong to eat meat is thus to deny there's any such choice to be made. After all, abstaining from meat is compatible with most other forms of activism. So, one might argue, the real choice is not between vegetarianism and participation in other causes; rather, it's between participating in various causes *while eating meat* or participating in them *while abstaining from meat*. If we're good people, the argument might go, we should opt for doing both.[16]

In support of this objection, we may note an important respect in which vegetarianism actually makes it *easier* to support other causes. Since vegetarian foods are often less expensive, people who avoid meat save money that they can then use to support other worthy causes. Far from facing a choice between vegetarianism and other forms of activism, people who contribute to other causes may actually be able to use vegetarianism as a tool for making more progress on the world's other problems.

These points are correct as far as they go. However, taking them as proof of an obligation to avoid meat implies an outlook on activism that's much more radical than vegetarians likely intend. For notice that it's possible to say of nearly everything we consume that doing without it would contribute to a valuable cause and save us money we could devote to other worthy causes as well. If we stopped comfortably heating and cooling our homes, for example, this would help fight climate change and mitigate toxic pollution while simultaneously reducing our utility bills. If we stopped buying new clothes and discarding worn-out items, this would help reduce waste and save resources while also shrinking our clothing expenditures. Even fresh fruits and vegetables can often be linked to important problems like groundwater depletion, shipping pollution, and the exploitation of laborers, such that giving them up would contribute to valuable causes, and the money we'd save by switching to a diet of less expensive starches (e.g., rice, potatoes, bread) and legumes (e.g., beans, lentils, split peas) could then be sent off to support other valuable causes as well.

Some readers may think this kind of self-denial is the only appropriate response to our problem-ridden world. However, I take it that the dialectic between vegetarians and meat-eaters is not simply a debate over whether *any* unnecessary consumption is acceptable. The question is whether eating meat is *specifically* wrong in a way that doesn't extend to, say, heating one's home, buying a t-shirt, or purchasing an expensive container of kiwifruit. With apologies to any ascetics reading this book, let's thus adopt the assumption (made widely by vegetarians and meat-eaters alike) that activists may legitimately say "Enough is enough" long before they've sacrificed everything short of necessities to their causes.

If we grant there's a limit on what we can expect people to sacrifice in response to the world's problems, this presents us with difficult decisions about how to proceed. For one thing, there's a question of how far we need to go before this limit is reached. The world's problems are vast and grave—far more important than our personal comfort, convenience, and enjoyment. Still, at least for most people, it's not as if making more sacrifices will *solve* these massive problems. Generally, the places where we can make the most discernible differences involve relatively modest problems in our own communities. For the bigger issues, we mostly face opportunities to contribute to movements where the marginal impacts of our personal contributions are negligible or hard to assess. (The latter is the case with vegetarianism.) Setting the right level of ambition in this context is difficult, but it's something each of us must do nonetheless.

There's also a question of *how* to contribute. There are opportunities to help with time, energy, patience, kindness, money, possessions, voice, creativity, and intellect, among many other things. Is it the right idea to give a bit of each of these? Is it better to specialize in a few ways of contributing? For example, can donating lots of money be a substitute for devoting time and energy? May a tireless volunteer keep their money without guilt? If a person takes a career in public service, can extraordinary devotion at work count as doing one's part?

These and many other puzzles stack atop the crucial question of which causes to support. The world is filled with problems crying out for attention, and it would be little use to try to impact all of them. Spreading ourselves thinly across as many causes as possible would virtually guarantee we'd fail to accomplish anything worthwhile for any of them. If you think of the people you regard as your heroes, you'll likely see that all of them focus their attention on some subset of worthy causes. Following their lead would inevitably mean leaving many problems unaddressed, but which causes should you focus on, and which will be the ones you ignore?

It's hard to say from the armchair how we should make these challenging determinations. Plausibly, no formula I could offer as a theorist would substitute for careful reflection and judgment. Yet, even if we lack a fully universal account of ethical activism, we can still say with confidence that people may permissibly decline to participate in innumerable activities and causes. This is not because it would be *impossible* to take on these activities, but simply because there's a limit on what we can reasonably expect people to do. Responsible activists will not try to be everything to everyone. Instead, they will select certain ways of contributing to certain causes to certain extents, recognizing there will always be more they could have done to advance causes they value and respect.

If all this is correct, we can see why it's not enough to say people *could* become vegetarians while also promoting other causes. People who become vegetarians tackle a certain set of problems in a certain way, and they do so by making certain sacrifices. This form of activism is compatible with—and even conducive to—promoting other causes as well. Yet, one can grant all this without conceding that it's wrong to eat meat. We can describe many forms of activism in just the same ways, and yet the fact remains we must choose which of these things we will do—which causes we wish to advance, by what means, and at what cost.

It's important to note in this connection that *even* if one decided to contribute to the aims of the vegetarian movement by abstaining from meat, one could clearly do this without becoming a vegetarian. For example, one could embrace a tradition of "Meatless Mondays," pay more attention to vegetarian options at restaurants, develop and publicize vegetarian recipes, or make a point of incorporating meat alternatives into one's cooking. It's also possible to contribute to the same general causes advanced by vegetarianism through entirely different kinds of action. For example, one could seek out producers whose operations meet higher standards of ethical accountability, donate to farm animal welfare organizations, or contribute to the campaigns of political candidates who stand up for animals, workers, the environment, and public health.

Crucially, however, this outlook also suggests it's possible to conscientiously allocate one's activist efforts among competing causes without doing any of these things. If a person took suitably ambitious actions on other problems, they could seemingly look vegetarians in the eye and say, "It's not that I deny your movement is important. I've just chosen to focus my efforts in other areas." To show the flaw in this kind of reasoning, vegetarians would need a different kind of argument than we've encountered thus far.

Although many causes vie for our attention as activists, some vegetarians may still want to insist theirs stands out as a distinctively compelling option for making an impact. If we think back to the restaurant example from earlier, the fact that you had an obligation to feed your child didn't obviously entail a duty to eat in a specific restaurant. But suppose we add details to the example so this restaurant is clearly the most prudent way to satisfy your duty. Imagine they offer delicious and healthy meals at highly affordable prices along with great service and a pleasant dining environment. The nearby competitors either serve far less appealing food or charge much higher prices. Unfortunately, you didn't remember to pack any food of your own. You're far from home. The nearest grocery store is several miles away. In this scenario, it might still not be true that you're literally *obligated* to eat at this restaurant—for example, you could suffer through a bad meal, pay excessively for your food, or subject yourself to a long car ride with a miserable child—but refusing to eat at the restaurant would seem silly, if not irrational. Given that the restaurateur is clearly offering you the best "bang for the buck" in the circumstances, you ought to take them up on their offer, all things considered. Turning back to the issue at hand, it's worth asking whether something similar can be said about vegetarianism.

Two kinds of consideration might be deployed to support such a claim. On the one hand, vegetarians might argue avoiding meat is especially easy as far as activist contributions go. Vegetarianism doesn't require people to march in the street or navigate tricky political processes (at least not inherently). It doesn't require sacrificing large sums of money (as we've said, it's generally cheaper than eating meat). In fact, vegetarianism doesn't require people to do much of anything they're not already doing in some form. We already face decisions about what to eat when we go to a restaurant, shop at the supermarket, or open the refrigerator. Vegetarianism simply asks us to make those decisions in ways that avoid meat. In the scheme of things, this might seem like a pretty simple and low-cost way to help make a difference.

On the other hand, vegetarians may also note their movement tackles some of the gravest problems in existence.[17] Recall that in 2020, US producers delivered 35.1 million cows, 139.4 million pigs, and 9.25 billion broiler chickens to market.[18] If we grant that a significant proportion of these animals endured serious harm along the way, then the total scale of the suffering is vast. Moreover, this isn't even the whole of the problem. The figures just listed are only for the United States—hardly the only country where animals are mistreated. And they don't include all the animals involved in domestic meat production (including, for example, those that die before their appointed time and breeding animals that aren't subsequently eaten). Recall also the other complaints about worker exploitation, environmental degradation, and public health endangerment. (Global climate change is a particularly enormous problem that's influenced considerably by meat production.) When one becomes a vegetarian, one contributes to a movement that's fighting all these critical problems.

Insofar as vegetarianism offers a pathway for tackling gargantuan problems through low-cost actions, it might seem to stand out as potentially the most prudent option available for tackling the world's ills. Anyone who chose not to take up this option and focused entirely on alternative forms of activism might thus seem to face an uphill battle in explaining why that choice made sense. On closer inspection, however, the value proposition offered by vegetarianism is far less decisive than the preceding arguments make it seem. In truth, it's not at all obvious vegetarianism represents a particularly low-cost form of activism, and it's likewise unclear it represents a uniquely efficacious way to make a difference in the world.

Let's start with the claim that vegetarianism is easy relative to other forms of activism. Surely there are some people for whom this characterization is correct. For example, some people find meat disgusting. Others live around so many vegetarians that avoiding meat is no trouble. For people like these, the absence of competing considerations makes vegetarianism a salient and attractive choice for their portfolio of activist efforts.

Yet, giving up meat is not so appealing for many other people. For one thing, taking up vegetarianism typically requires a reorientation in one's relationship with food. Many meat-eaters are accustomed to navigating the world without treating every meal as a weighty ethical decision. For them, adopting a commitment to vegetarianism would mean going through life in a different way, requiring significant investments of attention and willpower. New vegetarians must also relearn how to maintain their nutrition, cook for themselves, preserve variety in their diets, and navigate the restaurant world, among many other things.

The widespread existence of other meat-eaters is another source of difficulties. Meat-eaters are not always great about accommodating plant-based diets, and vegetarians often face pushback from friends, relatives, and colleagues. Especially among those who consider food a crucial tool for bringing people together and see meat as playing a central role in this, vegetarians' refusal to share in certain kinds of meals can generate significant social friction.[19]

We must also acknowledge that many meat-eaters genuinely enjoy eating meat. Most meat-eaters can think of certain instances of meat-eating that are deeply meaningful to them (e.g., turkey on Thanksgiving). But even many less important instances of meat-eating are enjoyable, and vegetarianism requires sacrificing them all.

Far from being a distinctly easy way to contribute to a good cause, vegetarianism thus commonly comes with significant burdens. Indeed, the existence of these burdens helps explain why, as I noted earlier, the vast majority of people who experiment with vegetarianism eventually return to eating meat.[20] There may be some people for whom such burdens are negligible or nonexistent, and for these people, the case for vegetarianism may indeed be strong. But for many meat-eaters, becoming a vegetarian would be quite costly relative to many of their other options for helping to make the world a better place.

Of course, vegetarianism's costliness might not be decisive if this form of activism made an outsized impact on the world. Insofar as we do have a duty to make certain sacrifices to contribute to valuable causes, these burdens might be warranted if vegetarianism were especially efficacious. Here too, however, things are not as clear as they might initially seem.

For one thing, although vegetarians tackle enormous problems, the scale of the problems themselves is not what's relevant to assessing the movement's efficacy. Rather, what matters is how much impact vegetarianism has on these problems and how that impact might grow with additional participants. By this measure, the case for characterizing vegetarianism as uniquely efficacious seems murky. Despite decades of effort from millions of people willing to make significant lifestyle changes to promote their cause, most of the problems vegetarians tackle have shown little improvement over time. The amount of unethically produced meat consumed around the world has grown and is projected to continue growing.[21] Meat industry workers continue to endure harsh conditions and powerlessness. Environmental degradation remains a serious global problem. And as I write this book in 2021, the continued public health risks associated with meat are on powerful display from a pandemic coronavirus with an animal origin. Although vegetarians have certainly helped make these problems less severe than they would have been otherwise, the massive scale of the remaining challenges is hardly evidence of vegetarianism's unparalleled efficacy.

There's a structural reason, too, why we should expect vegetarianism to be less than completely successful in promoting its aims. Although vegetarians engage in many forms of activism aside from avoiding meat, their primary and most characteristic tool is the consumer boycott.[22] As a general rule, boycotts work because they promise to *end*: activists and their allies refuse to consume products unless certain demands are met, and it's the prospect of regaining consumers that incentivizes producers to change their behavior. Yet, it's in vegetarianism's nature that there's no offer on the table to resume consuming the meat industry's products. Short of simply abandoning their operations, there's nothing meat producers can do to regain patronage from vegetarians.[23] Thus, rather than pressuring producers to adopt better practices, vegetarian boycotts serve mainly to withdraw some amount of revenue from a multi-billion-dollar industry with a broad, loyal, and growing global customer base.

My purpose in making these comments is not to disparage vegetarians' important and valuable accomplishments. Rather, it's simply to undermine the claim that vegetarianism is such a peerless form of activism that every responsible person has a decisive reason to take it up. Given vegetarians' limited success in achieving their goals and the questionable wisdom of their core strategy for action, it seems fair to think that a person could decide to prioritize other forms of activism without clearly getting worse "bang for the buck."

Pushing back on this conclusion once again, some vegetarians might emphasize that their efforts don't revolve *exclusively* around boycotting meat. For example, many vegetarians are actively involved in promoting political reforms that would end the meat industry's most serious abuses. Many also go out of their way to support products like lab-grown tissues or plant-based meat alternatives with the potential to make meat production obsolete someday. However, emphasizing these alternative forms of vegetarian activism actually reinforces my point. It's entirely possible to advocate politically for meat industry reforms without becoming a vegetarian.[24] Indeed, in some political circles, a willingness to eat meat might actually be an asset since vegetarians are often viewed as ideological outsiders.[25] Likewise, it's possible to support and promote meat alternatives while also eating meat: in fact, some 98% of the people who consume these products fall into this category.[26] By attending to all the ways people can help advance similar objectives without abstaining from meat, we once again invite the question of why vegetarianism is *specifically* required instead of just one of many options for helping make the world a better place.

A MISGUIDED ARGUMENTATIVE STRATEGY

This chapter began with an intuitively powerful argument for why the meat industry's harmful behavior makes it wrong to consume its products. Meat production is linked to a variety of serious problems. Since the meat industry survives because people buy its products, meat-eaters play a central role in sustaining the industry's wrongs. It may thus have initially seemed that people ought to stop eating meat to help eliminate these problems.

As we've seen, however, establishing this conclusion is far from straightforward. As individuals, our consumption decisions generally make no difference to how the meat industry operates. Thus, if the idea is that meat-eating is wrong because when a person eats meat, they cause bad things to happen, then *that* argument won't go through on factual grounds.

A more plausible version of the argument zooms out to the level of the vegetarian *movement* and examines the effects of many people avoiding meat as part of a coordinated strategy. Even though no vegetarian can claim credit for having *personally* created the benefits produced by the movement, there's no denying vegetarians have made a positive *collective* impact across numerous dimensions. Since these benefits only arise because individuals are willing to do their part to contribute to them, this provides some reason for us to become vegetarians.

However, the problem with this revised argument is that there are many causes with similar claims to producing valuable impacts through the contributions of many individuals. Although we are plausibly obligated to participate in at least some of these causes, no one is required to participate in all of them. And vegetarianism doesn't appear to be the sort of uniquely low-cost/high-impact option that would make it stand out as obviously the most prudent way to focus one's efforts. All of this suggests a person can adequately fulfill their moral duty to contribute to valuable causes without specifically giving up meat—and, indeed, without taking any action to address the meat issue more generally.

For some readers, conceding this point may seem like the end of the conversation, such that we can now conclude it's OK to eat meat. But this would be too hasty, for as we'll see in the next two chapters, there are other arguments for vegetarianism that don't require making any of the claims rebutted in this chapter. The upshot so far is only that one family of vegetarian arguments—i.e., that which connects the duty to avoid meat to the importance of impacting the meat industry—is unpersuasive. If eating meat is wrong, vegetarians need another way to show it.

There's a second more important limitation to this chapter's arguments as well. Over the last few pages, I've been contending that people have considerable latitude in choosing which causes to support and what actions to take to participate in those causes. However, for almost every meat-eater reading this book, it's simply not true that you're choosing not to become a vegetarian because you've focused your efforts on other forms of activism.[27] In a world full of serious problems, most of us are falling short of what we ought to be doing to help make things better, even by our own standards.

If you fall into this category of being a meat-eater who's not doing enough, then you have good reason to feel guilty when vegetarians implore you to join them. Every time you put a piece of meat in your mouth, you're failing to take an opportunity to help make the world a better place—and not because you already feel you've done enough. If my arguments in this chapter have been correct, then this specific opportunity is not one you have a duty to prioritize over all the other causes you could take up instead. But if you *don't* take up some of those other causes to an extent you consider adequate, then it's appropriate for you to feel guilty. It's appropriate to feel guilty about eating meat—and about not standing up for those victimized by injustice, not donating to help those in need, not supporting needed research, and not doing countless other things you could be doing but aren't. The arguments of this chapter defend *focusing* on certain issues and actions. They offer no defense for indifference or laziness in responding to our problem-filled world.

Five

For many vegetarians, the case against meat-eating revolves around the meat industry's operations. Mainstream meat production is linked to serious concerns about animal mistreatment, worker exploitation, and public health endangerment. These problems, in turn, derive from the fact people purchase and consume meat. Because of the connection between meat-eaters' diets and serious moral wrongs, vegetarians have often concluded the only ethical course of action is to avoid meat altogether.

The previous chapter showed it's difficult to establish this conclusion by claiming that when a person eats meat, they marginally worsen the meat industry's problems, whereas abstaining would cause the problems to become marginally less severe. That line of argument rested on a factual mistake: in practice, dietary choices at the scale of an individual consumer don't materially affect the industry's operations at all. We saw it's possible to rescue some sense of efficacy by stepping back and examining vegetarians' impacts on a collective level. But from that vantage point, vegetarianism looked like just one of many ways to participate in cooperative efforts to tackle serious problems. Whatever duties we have to respond to the world's ills, they don't obligate us to participate in every praiseworthy

123 **What If Everyone Did That?**

DOI: 10.4324/9781003221944-5

movement or take up every valuable cause. Focusing on veg-etarians' collective impacts helps show why vegetarianism is an *option*—perhaps even a *good* option—for fulfilling our duty to help make the world a better place. Yet, this way of arguing makes vegetarianism look like something we may legitimately decline to take up in favor of focusing on other causes.

The last chapter concluded that it is an unpromising strat-egy to try to vindicate vegetarianism by appealing to its causal impacts. However, this is hardly a death knell for ethical veg-etarianism. As we'll see over the next two chapters, there are many other rationales for abstaining from meat that don't revolve around claims of causal potency. These arguments hold eating meat is wrong for reasons other than its direct impacts, and thus good people will be vegetarians regardless of the difference this makes to the outcomes we achieve.

In what follows, I'll distinguish between two groups of such arguments. One group, which I'll wait to discuss until the next chapter, considers how our eating decisions shape our position in the world—what we stand for, how we take responsibility for problems we've helped create, how dirty our hands are, and how we feel about our actions. In this chapter, I'll focus on a different group of arguments. These examine meat-eating not simply as a single person's choice but rather as a *kind* of action we can assess according to its generalized results.

This chapter's title captures one intuitive way to understand what this second group of arguments is doing. Instead of ask-ing, "What happens when *you* eat meat," or "what happens when *you* become vegetarian," the question is, "What happens if people *generally* behave as you do?" These arguments hold the answer to this latter question can illuminate our actions' rightness or wrongness in a way that doesn't depend on the effects of our specific choices at any point in time.

In the coming pages, I'll argue that regardless of whether we press this kind of question with an eye to how meat-eaters behave or how vegetarians do, we won't establish that eating meat is wrong. If we think of meat-eaters as not just meat-eaters but also as people choosing to allocate their efforts to other causes (as we discussed in the previous chapter), then generalizing their behavior wouldn't generate unacceptable results. Likewise, if we think of vegetarianism as a way of adhering to rules that *would be* desirable if generally followed—even though only a tiny proportion of people follow them in practice—then the case for avoiding meat is unclear as well. As with the previous chapter's discussion, the upshot of this analysis will not yet be that it's OK to eat meat since there remain other objections to consider. But once again, we'll see that an intuitive strategy for defending vegetarianism proves unsuccessful, and hence a different approach is needed if ethical vegetarians hope to vindicate their view.

THE UNIVERSALIZATION TEST

An influential tradition in moral philosophy holds that a crucial test of an ethical principle is whether it can survive *universalization*.[1] This test instructs us to envision what it would be like if everyone (or nearly everyone) followed the principle we're considering and ask whether we could will such a world into being. If the answer is yes, our principle passes the test. However, it's easy to see why the answer might turn out to be no.

Often, when we're tempted to engage in immoral behavior, what's actually going on is that *we* want to be able to do a certain kind of thing, but we want *others* to refrain from following our lead. Consider a person who's tempted to steal.

No one wants to live in a world where everyone steals whenever they like. What the thief desires is to steal while others generally do not. By exposing the thief's actions to the test of universalization, we get the clear and correct result that this behavior is immoral.

There are different ways the universalization test can pronounce a principle unacceptable. In some instances, attempting to universalize a particular behavior yields a kind of incoherence. Consider promise-breaking, for example. If everyone adopted the principle of breaking promises whenever keeping them was inconvenient, the very act of "promising" would become unintelligible. If every time a person said, "I promise to …," you knew they would only honor their pledge if it suited them at the moment, the word "promise" would lose its meaning. At best, "I promise to …" might mean something like "I expect to …" or "I would like to think I will …" But there wouldn't be any promising in the usual sense.

In other instances, universal adoption of a bad principle would be coherent but nevertheless awful. The case of theft illustrates this. If everyone knew others were prepared to steal whenever they liked, life would be much worse. But there's nothing incoherent about such a world: each thief would face the prospect that whatever they stole could just as easily be taken from them, but such a world is certainly intelligible. It's just that no one would want to live in that world when they had the option of living in one more like ours, where people generally don't steal even when they might benefit from doing so.

A WORLD FULL OF MEAT-EATERS

Intuitively, the universalization test might seem to provide a straightforward way to see that it's wrong to eat meat produced as most of ours is.[2] As I've said throughout this book, widespread consumption of meat industry products drives animal mistreatment, worker exploitation, environmental degradation, and public health endangerment on a massive scale. It's because most people embrace the principle that they'll eat meat whenever they like that these terrible problems exist. If everyone adopted vegetarian principles instead, the meat industry's problems would disappear. The case for vegetarianism might seem to be open-and-shut if we accept universalization as the right way to test moral principles.[3]

To show what's wrong with this line of reasoning, it'll help to begin by observing that, whatever we think of the universalization test as a general tool for ethical reasoning, it's nevertheless susceptible to producing misleading results. In particular, simply asking, "What if everyone did that," can make lots of permissible actions look impermissible if we're not careful to specify the form of conduct to be tested. Take, for example, the act of launching a career as a hospital nurse. Presumably, this is a permissible and even admirable thing to do. But what if *everyone* took a career as a hospital nurse? Who would grow food? Who would staff factories, power stations, and schools? Who, indeed, would build hospitals for these nurses or produce their scrubs, equipment, and medicines? Not only would a world full of hospital nurses degenerate into chaos and death, but it's not even clear what it would *mean* to call someone a "hospital nurse" in a world without hospitals, nursing schools, and countless other inputs to the practice of nursing.

Obviously, the upshot of this example is not that it's impermissible to become a nurse. Rather, something has clearly gone wrong with the universalization test itself. In fact, what's happened is that by focusing too narrowly on the act of *becoming a hospital nurse*, we've lost sight of how nurses' behavior fits into a broader division of labor in which nurses work alongside others who occupy countless different social roles. The explanation for why it's OK to become a nurse is not that *everyone* should become a nurse; rather, it's that nursing plays a valuable role in our complex economic system. When we reframe our question to capture this broader context, the problem goes away—asking, "What if *everyone* took a beneficial job in the economy?" enables us to see how people could generally act on this principle without issue.

This same point can be extended to attempts to universalize things people *don't* do as well. Keeping with the same example, we can observe that someone who pursues a career as a nurse will likely not become a farmer. Someone might say, "What if *nobody* farmed? That would be disastrous!" But although this is true, it would be wrong to infer that anyone who declines to farm is misbehaving. When we focus narrowly on specific things people *don't* do—and ignore the other valuable things they choose to do instead—we can easily make the mistake of thinking they're behaving unethically. Once again, it's only by stepping back and considering how diverse actions can fit *together* that we can appreciate the value of each individual's distinctive contributions.

The previous chapter's discussion should prime us to wonder whether problems like these could arise when using the universalization test to condemn meat-eating. A key idea in that earlier discussion was that there are far more problems in the world than any individual can realistically tackle, and thus each of us faces hard choices about how to focus our efforts. I suggested that if we think of vegetarianism as a strategy for tackling an important problem, it will look like just one of many such strategies. Returning to our current discussion, we may find vegetarianism comes out looking analogous to nursing—that is, like just one of many possible ways to fit oneself into broader social efforts to make the world a better place.

According to this analysis, applying the universalization test to meat-eaters *as such* involves the same mistake as applying it to "non-farmers." If a non-farmer is nothing more than a non-farmer, we might well criticize them for failing to contribute to the social division of labor. But if the non-farmer is a nurse, such criticism would be misguided. Likewise, if a meat-eater is *only* a meat-eater—that is, if all they do in the face of the world's problems is to go on eating meat—then, as I said in the previous chapter, they certainly deserve to be criticized. But if the meat-eater is an ardent contributor to other forms of action, the criticism is less clearly valid. If we universalize the principle behind the outlook of our earlier discussion, it's far from obvious such a world could not be willed into existence. Would it really be impossible to embrace a world in which each person energetically took up some subset of causes, leaving others to be taken up by other people? For what it's worth, I would be happy to live in a world like that.

A WORLD FULL OF VEGETARIANS

If we try to use the universalization test to see what's so bad about meat-eaters, the exercise will turn up inconclusive. As long as meat-eaters aren't *only* meat-eaters—that is, if they decline to become vegetarians because they've decided to focus on other causes instead—then it's not clear universalizing their behavior would yield unacceptable results. A world full of people tackling diverse causes in many different ways isn't obviously objectionable. Indeed, the vision of such a world may even be inspiring.

Still, one may deny that this settles whether the universalization test can vindicate vegetarianism. For suppose we shift our focus away from what meat-eaters do and consider vegetarians' actions instead. If everyone abstained from meat, this would eliminate many important problems. In an ideal world, *no one* would buy and eat meat produced like most is today. Thus, when people eat meat, they do something they have good reason to wish *no one* would do. On the face of it, this looks like just the sort of corrupt behavior we discussed earlier, whereby people make exceptions for themselves to rules they wish others would follow.

For the sake of discussion, let's grant that if we lived in a world where no one (or virtually no one) ate meat that had been produced in objectionable ways, then we should abstain as well. In that world, consumers of unethically produced meat would undermine a valuable cooperative arrangement that was successfully resolving important problems, and such behavior seems wrong.[4] But how does this bear on what we should do in our world, where the vast majority of people *do* eat this meat and we lack effective arrangements to eliminate the meat industry's problems? The appeal to an ideal meat-free world forces us to confront an important question. What's the relationship between how people would behave in an ideal world and how *we* ought to behave in our non-ideal reality?[5]

IDEAL OUTCOMES VS. STRATEGIC DECISIONS

To work toward an answer, let's begin by demonstrating that it's at least *possible* for there to be a difference between the actions that would be best in an ideal world and the ones we should actually take in practice. Suppose, for example, that we learned there are significant advantages to having everyone drive on the left side of the road. In this case, we could accurately say that, in an ideal world, everyone would drive on the left, and it would be objectionable to drive on the right. These claims notwithstanding, it seems clear that for those of us who live in countries like the United States where people drive on the right, speculations about how people would drive in an ideal world have no bearing on what we ought to do in practice. Even if people *would ideally* drive on the left, we should still drive on the right since that's what we generally expect others to do.

As a way to help us think more clearly about this example and others like it, it'll be helpful to equip ourselves with some tools from the science of strategic interaction known as game theory.[6] Put simply, game theory offers a framework for thinking about situations in which outcomes depend not just on one person's actions but rather on combinations of actions taken by independent decision makers. Within this framework, a "game" is simply an interactive situation involving multiple individuals (called "players") who must choose among alternative courses of actions (called "moves") that combine to produce outcomes for each individual (called "payoffs").

To illustrate how this framework operates, let's look again at the example of selecting a side of the road for driving. Imagine you and I are driving toward each other on a country road in the middle of the night. In keeping with what I said earlier, suppose we both believe that, in an ideal world, everyone would drive on the left instead of the right. However, what we both value most is aligning our driving behavior with what the other is doing. If I were to bear to my left while you bore to your right—or vice versa—the result would be a head-on collision.

We can depict this situation using a matrix like the one in Figure 5.1. In this chart, each quadrant corresponds to one possible combination of our driving choices. The upper left-hand quadrant represents the outcome where both of us drive on the left. The label in the lower left-hand corner of the box represents the "payoff" of this outcome from my perspective: of all the possible outcomes, this is the one I prefer most. The label in the upper right-hand corner represents the "payoff" for you: in your eyes, having us both drive on the left is the best outcome, too. Meanwhile, the lower right-hand quadrant corresponds to the outcome where we both decide to drive on the right side of the road. As the labels convey, both of us regard this as the second-best possible outcome—not as good as the ideal solution, but still good insofar as we coordinate our behavior and thus avoid a collision. The lower left-hand and upper right-hand quadrants both represent outcomes in which each of us makes a different choice from the other. In the upper right-hand quadrant, I've decided to drive on my left and you on your right, causing us to crash. In the lower left-hand quadrant, it's you on your left and me on my right, creating the same problem. As the labels convey, both of these outcomes are undesirable.

		You	
		Drive on Left	Drive on Right
Me	Drive on Left	1st best 1st best	3rd best 3rd best
	Drive on Right	3rd best 3rd best	2nd best 2nd best

Figure 5.1 Pure Coordination Game.

In addition to providing a general illustration of how game theory works, this example helps make clear why the most sensible course of action in the real world can sometimes come apart from what would be ideal. Even if the best outcome in this situation would be for us to both drive on our left, it still pays for me to keep to my right if that's what I expect you to do. Likewise, if you expect me to drive on my right, you'd better do that as well. It's not enough to make a compelling case for either of us to drive on our left to show that it would be *ideal* if we both did that. There would need to be adequate reason for each of us to expect the other to follow suit.

When we're just thinking about two people making a decision that affects both of them, it might seem intuitive to think they should be able to figure things out so that everyone gets what they want most. But often, real-life situations aren't so simple. If you're driving down a road in the middle of the night, you may not be able to stop and have a conversation with an oncoming driver about your respective driving decisions. More generally, in a country like the United States where people have been driving on the right side of the road for decades, getting people to change their driving behavior is no simple task. Even if the vast majority of people came to believe it would be better to have everyone drive on the left, we would still expect them to keep driving on the right unless something major happened (e.g., the passage of a new law). Because each person would reasonably expect others to keep driving on the right due to long established norms, no one individual would have reason to change their behavior and suddenly start driving on the left. In fact, in that kind of scenario, unilaterally switching sides of the road wouldn't be a good way to express one's commitment to ideal conduct: it would be a way to get people seriously hurt.

This scenario's structure has a name among game theorists: the "Pure Coordination Game." (It's a "coordination" game because our overriding interest is in coordinating our actions with one another's. It's a "pure" coordination game because we share a common interest in coordinating on one of our options over any other.) The case of picking a side of the road is just one kind of scenario that exhibits this structure; it's possible to identify many others that share the same general arrangement of options and payoffs. Game theorists have examined other kinds of strategic situations as well, giving them such colorful names as "Chicken," the "Dictator Game," and the "Prisoner's Dilemma."

CHASING STAGS

For thinking about the ethics of eating meat, there's a particularly relevant form of interaction known by game theorists as the "Stag Hunt."[7] To understand the structure of this game, imagine there are two hunters out trying to get meat to feed their families. (For the sake of the example, ignore whether hunting is ethical and suppose it's important for each to succeed.) Each hunter's standard operating procedure—which works virtually without fail—is to hide quietly in a tree until a hare (i.e., rabbit) happens past, at which point they use their bow and arrow to kill it and take it home. On this day, however, the hunters each spot a large stag (i.e., male deer) in the distance that could provide a much better meal than any hare. But there's a problem. The hunters would need to work together to capture the stag, pursuing it from opposite directions to make its escape more difficult. Yet, the hunters are currently hiding some distance apart from each other. They can't communicate without alerting the forest animals to their presence, and neither can verify whether the other is joining the chase for the stag or staying put to hunt hare. Pursuing the stag thus presents a risk: if one hunter chases the stag while the other sticks with the hare, then the stag-chasing hunter will go home empty-handed. By contrast, hunting hare is basically risk-free. Each hunter can capture a hare regardless of the other's actions, making this is a surefire way for each to guarantee food for their family.

We can depict the hunters' situation through the matrix in Figure 5.2. As in the Pure Coordination Game, the best outcome for both hunters is in the upper left-hand quadrant, where both decide to hunt stag and take home an excellent meal. A second-best outcome is once again in the lower right-hand corner, with both hunters playing it safe and hunting hare. But unlike in the Pure Coordination Game, a hunter who plays it safe and opts for hare is unaffected by the other's choice. Although coordination is essential for anyone who would chase the stag, a hunter who chooses hare does not need to worry about coordinating at all.

My description of the Stag Hunt imbues each hunter's decision with the character of a dilemma: "Should I take the risk of going home empty-handed for a chance at the stag? Should I opt instead for the sure thing?" The answers to such questions

Hunter 2

		Hunt Stag	Hunt Hare
Hunter 1	Hunt Stag	1st best 1st best	2nd best 3rd best
	Hunt Hare	3rd best 2nd best	2nd best 2nd best

Figure 5.2 Stag Hunt.

would seem to depend on several variables. For example, how much better is it to have stag rather than hare? How bad is it to end up with nothing?

Once again, however, things change when we build background expectations into the story. Suppose this isn't the first time these hunters have encountered a stag in the woods, and pretty much every time this happens, one of the hunters decides to play it safe and hunt hare. How should the other hunter respond to this? Even if they wish the other hunter would be more willing to take chances on stags, it would be silly for them to base their decision on this hypothetical ideal. Given what this hunter has every reason to expect the other to do, the best move is to stay put and hunt hare. This, in turn, reinforces the other hunter's rationale for hunting hare as well.

Like the Pure Coordination Game, the Stag Hunt helps us see how people can get stuck in suboptimal situations because of how they expect others to behave. In contrast to that earlier example, however, the hunters in the Stag Hunt don't choose to hunt hare because they've settled on a system of cooperation according to which anyone who hunts stag will harm others. Unlike driving on a different side of the road from what others expect, unilaterally chasing the stag is only harmful to the person who does it. Still, this self-destructiveness is a powerful reason not to chase stag while others hunt hare. Even if it would be better if *everyone* were willing to hunt stag together, a hunter surrounded by people who consistently hunt hare would be foolish to use this ideal as the basis for their choice.

Once again, these dynamics become even starker when we start incorporating additional hunters into the picture. If catching a stag depended on cooperation from many different hunters, and each hunter thought there was a considerable risk most of the others wouldn't show up, it's easy to see why a hunter spotting a distant stag might decide to stay put. Especially if a hunting community had a long history of failed stag hunts and many members openly resigned to eating hare, the ideal scenario of everyone coming together to capture a stag might hold little power to motivate anybody to act.

Dynamics like these aren't limited to hypothetical hunting scenarios. There are innumerable areas of life where, if only everyone would unite and do their part, incredible things could be accomplished—but where the overwhelming likelihood is that most people *won't* do their parts, and so the desired objective won't be realized. In situations like these, pointing to what would *ideally* happen may do little to motivate action, and not just because people are lazy, selfish, or uncaring. Even people who would be happy to do their part *so long as others did so as well* may sensibly refuse to "hunt stag" when they expect their neighbors to stick with "hunting hare."

The dynamics of the Stag Hunt seem clearly relevant to our investigation regarding the ethics of eating meat. Given the gravity of the meat industry's ills, it would seem highly desirable to live in a world where these problems disappeared due to everyone abstaining from conventionally produced meat. However, in our world, we don't get to choose on our own whether to realize that ideal. The choice we face is whether to eat meat when we know the vast majority of our neighbors will eat it or whether to abstain alongside a comparatively tiny contingent of others. We can't settle the best decision in *that* scenario simply by pointing to the ideal in which everyone agrees to abstain. We are like a hunter who spots a stag but knows their neighbors are resolved to hunt hares. To decide the best course of action, we need to account for the fact that, in our non-ideal circumstances, most people aren't vegetarians, and the meat industry's problems aren't being solved through voluntary cooperation with vegetarian norms.[8]

RAISING THE STAKES

Although the situation confronting would-be vegetarians bears clear structural similarities to the story of the Stag Hunt, there are also important differences worth noting. Perhaps most significantly, the hunters' story was framed solely in terms of individuals pursuing self-interest, whereas the meat issue is a matter of great moral importance. Even if one grants individuals are justified in "hunting hare" when what hangs in the balance is their personal or familial well-being, one may doubt whether they would be similarly justified if failing to coordinate on "hunting stag" would result in ethical tragedy.

To think clearly about the question of meat-eating, we need to move away from imaginary stories of deer hunting (a controversial enterprise in itself) and take up scenarios in which failure to coordinate results in morally serious harm. Let's thus consider the problem of smog pollution. In the 1960s, many American cities experienced major problems with smog—a thick haze of air pollution that aggravated heart and lung problems and increased cancer rates. Much of this smog was caused by automobile emissions, which reacted with sunlight to form pollutants that could remain aloft for days. The hazards from smog pollution rose to the level of a public health crisis in some areas.

Eventually, a technology was developed to solve the smog problem. Catalytic converters used chemical reactions to neutralize harmful substances in car exhaust before they were released. The converters had drawbacks, however. They were expensive to build and install, they severely reduced cars' performance, and they didn't work well with the standard formulations of gasoline available at the time. But despite their downsides, regulators eventually took action to promote their spread, requiring automobile manufacturers to install them in cars built after 1975 and pushing gas companies to offer more compatible fuel formulations. These reforms helped reduce smog to tolerable levels in many American cities.[9]

Imagine if history had unfolded differently, however. Suppose governments had declined to promote catalytic converters through regulatory interventions and instead left citizens to decide whether to adopt them independently. In this situation, each citizen would have faced a choice: "Should I install a catalytic converter or go on driving without one?"

On the face of things, it would seem sensible for citizens to reason through their alternatives in much the same way as the people in the Stag Hunt scenario. We might suppose for the sake of discussion that each citizen agrees smog is a serious problem and would be willing to bear the costs of installing and using a catalytic converter *if their neighbors were generally doing so as well*. But if others weren't installing catalytic converters, it's not clear why any given citizen should feel a duty to adopt one unilaterally. Installing and operating a catalytic converter would come with a variety of costs, inconveniences, and hardships—and reducing a single car's emissions on the margin wouldn't make any noticeable difference to the local smog problem. Especially for someone who could imagine many other ways to tackle the world's problems, the hypothetical ideal of a smog-free society would hardly provide a definitive answer of what to do in a world filled with widespread non-cooperation.

This example helps us see that even when morally weighty outcomes are at stake, it's not always straightforward to infer *what you should actually do* by reflecting on *what would be best if everyone did it*.[10] If such situations have the structural characteristics of a Stag Hunt, we may find ourselves split between saying we *would* engage in cooperative behavior if we thought others would do so as well, but we *won't* take such actions when we don't expect others to follow suit. We can refer to this attitude as one of "conditional cooperation": we're happy to cooperate *only on the condition* that we can expect enough other people to cooperate as well.[11]

Even if we agree smog pollution is a serious problem and would readily cooperate if others were working together to solve it, that doesn't show we're obligated to take "cooperative" action when most others aren't doing so. It might seem like we can say something similar in the case of meat-eating as well. Even for those who accept the seriousness of the meat industry's problems and would readily cooperate in a social arrangement that eliminated them, it might not be obvious why it's obligatory to avoid meat when the vast majority of people continue eating it. Without further argument, an attitude of conditional cooperation seems defensible here as well.

TURNING THE TIDE

I've argued that even in the face of morally serious problems, it's OK to take the attitude of a "conditional cooperator." Such an attitude recommends participating in collective problem-solving efforts when it seems others will also participate, but it doesn't demand unilateral action when widespread cooperation appears unlikely.[12] However, there's an obvious objection to this line of thinking. If people generally approach problems as conditional cooperators, it stands to reason many problems will never get solved. Everyone will wait around for others to act first, expressing readiness to join cooperative schemes once they've been put in place but never *creating* those schemes when they don't already exist.

One might bolster this objection by pointing out that, whereas the simplified Stag Hunt framing makes cooperation look like an all-or-nothing affair, the real world is often more complicated. When it comes to solving actual problems, activists can achieve crucial gains even when most people aren't yet participating. The first "cooperators" who tackle a problem can make valuable partial progress toward addressing it and lay the groundwork for further efforts. As more people join them, the impact grows, and it becomes more appealing for others to get involved. Eventually, widespread cooperation can emerge when the bulk of the community "jumps on the bandwagon" of pioneering efforts like these.[13] It may therefore seem like morally exemplary people shouldn't simply be conditional cooperators. Instead, they should be the ones at the vanguard who get cooperation off the ground.[14]

There are some important kernels of truth in this line of argument. When social problems are solved by widespread cooperation, there must surely be individuals who take the first steps. And there's clearly something admirable about being one of these people. Insofar as vegetarians are undertaking an effort to cultivate a new form of cooperation around morally desirable norms, we should praise them for doing so.

However, there are two reasons why it's a mistake to reason from these kernels of truth to the conclusion that everyone must become vegetarian. The first is that activist efforts—even pioneering ones—don't always have to involve establishing new forms of cooperation. Voluntary adoption of new behavioral norms is just one of many ways of solving social problems. In the real-world case of smog pollution, the solution didn't come from people voluntarily installing catalytic converters: governments began mandating them, and non-compliance became a punishable offense. As we discussed in the previous chapter, we can find a similar diversity of strategies for addressing the meat issue as well. In addition to cultivating vegetarian norms, activists can push for regulatory reforms, technological breakthroughs, or new approaches to farming. Although widespread ethical vegetarianism is one way to solve the problems we face, it's hardly the only way, and it may not even be the most promising option.

The second problem with this line of reasoning is that, as I've said before, there are innumerable problems that could be solved if only everyone would cooperate. Even if there's some reason to try to become a pioneer in establishing cooperative solutions to problems, no one has a duty to do this in every situation in which cooperation is absent. This seems especially clear in contexts where there's strong reason to suspect pioneering efforts won't result in a cascading "bandwagon" effect. Suppose one learns, for example, that millions of "pioneers" have been trying for decades to create a new form of voluntary cooperation. However, they've so far failed to secure widespread compliance, and the vast majority of people who have tried to join their efforts have eventually reverted to their former non-cooperative behavior. (This is the situation with vegetarianism.) In such a case, the possibility of initiating a social cascade would seemingly need qualification against the overwhelming likelihood that no cascade will result from one's actions.

These considerations once again make vegetarianism look like one thing people may do to help make the world a better place but not something that they have a specific duty to do. Granted, a person who exploits the role of "conditional cooperator" to avoid doing anything about any problem is worthy of criticism for that fact. But there's no reason activist efforts—even pioneering ones—must always take the form of unilateral cooperation, and ethical activism certainly doesn't need to involve pioneering responses to every problem. It's therefore no objection to the analysis presented above that a world full of conditional cooperators would end up stagnating in unsolved problems. The world most certainly needs pioneers, but there's no apparent reason to think every activist—or even every pioneer—needs to be a vegetarian.

HOLDING SERVE

In an ideal world, no one would eat meat that had been produced the way most of ours is. Meanwhile, in our non-ideal reality, the meat industry's problems are perpetuated because many people do eat unethically produced meat. Intuitively, there might seem to be a direct connection between such statements and the conclusion that people ought to become vegetarians. If it would be morally desirable for no one to eat conventionally produced meat, and if its consumption yields terrible results, it might seem natural to think this just shows it's wrong to eat meat and vegetarianism is morally mandatory.

As we've seen in this chapter, however, things aren't so simple. The most straightforward strategy for establishing such a connection—the "universalization" test—turns out inconclusive for establishing the wrongness of eating meat. If we conceive of meat-eaters as only meat-eaters—and not as people who eschew vegetarianism to focus on other causes, as I've advocated—then the test indeed yields condemnation. However, when we take a more holistic outlook toward meateaters and their choices, it seems entirely acceptable to universalize the principles behind their behavior. A world full of people responding to problems through a diversity of pathways is hardly the sort of scenario to inspire deep moral disgust, to say the least.

If we focus instead on the actions of vegetarians, we can see in vegetarian activism a kind of cooperative behavior meat-eaters fail to exhibit. If everyone behaved with this sort of cooperativeness, the meat industry's problems would go away. Only because meat-eaters don't cooperate do these problems continue to exist. Again, however, these reflections don't vindicate the case for avoiding meat in a world where most people are not vegetarians and where the meat industry's problems are unlikely to be resolved anytime soon by voluntary cooperation. For people who eat meat, the structure of our present situation resembles what game theorists call a Stag Hunt. I've argued that in the face of a Stag Hunt, it's acceptable to take the attitude of a "conditional cooperator" who doesn't act when it's clear most others will neglect to follow suit. This is not to say we should *always* refuse to tackle problems until we know others will act: on the contrary, pioneering new forms of cooperation is a valuable and necessary form of activism. But responsible activism doesn't always have to take the form of unilateral cooperation, and even those who take up this form of action have no duty to do so for every cause where there's pioneering to be done.

Once again, we have found that an intuitive line of argument for ethical vegetarianism cannot stand up to scrutiny. Once again, vegetarianism has come out looking like a valuable thing we *may* do to combat important problems but not something we have a *specific duty* to take up. However, this is not the end of our investigation, for there remain arguments we have yet to consider. Let's thus move on to one last family of vegetarian arguments so we can finally assert that it's OK to eat meat.

Six

Our discussion thus far has tackled several important arguments for ethical vegetarianism. We've seen it's hard to vindicate a duty to avoid meat by appealing to vegetarianism's impacts on the world, and it likewise won't do to invoke claims about what the world would be like if everyone—or no one—behaved as meat-eaters do. In this chapter, we'll discuss one final family of vegetarian arguments having to do with how we position ourselves in the world.

As Jonathan Safran Foer observes, "When we lift our forks, we hang our hats somewhere. We set ourselves in one relationship or another to farmed animals, farm-workers, national economies, and global markets."[1] In Foer's view, and the views of many other vegetarians, meat-eating is wrong because of how it shapes our relationships with the meat industry's problems. If we believe meat producers' practices are unacceptable, it may fairly be asked: how can we keep buying and eating their products without standing in opposition to our own values?

Questions like these carry the suggestion that we ought to become vegetarians, not so much because of the difference it would make or because of some ideal set of rules it would comport with, but rather because it's independently important how we position ourselves toward wrongdoing. As Julia Driver puts the idea, "One ought to stand up for the good

DOI: 10.4324/9781003221944-6

and against the bad, and buying into a bad collective practice seems utterly opposed to this ideal."[2] This chapter will examine several arguments drawing on intuitions like these. By showing why they're misdirected, we'll set the stage for finally concluding that it's OK to eat meat.

TAKING A STAND

Cheshire Calhoun perceptively observes that being ethical isn't only about what *actions* we take; it's also about what we *stand* for.[3] People of integrity don't just privately adhere to their convictions; they also stand up for their values in a public way. This notion of "standing for something" is important for our discussion because, whereas the last two chapters suggested people can legitimately choose not to become vegetarians if they tackle society's problems in other ways, standing up for our values doesn't always seem like something we can shrug off just because we've behaved well in other respects. Even a person who takes admirable action on the world's problems may nevertheless seem lacking in integrity if, when faced with attacks on her deeply held convictions, she simply capitulates, keeps silent, or nods along with the crowd.

One way of applying this idea to our current conversation concerns the positions we take in discussion with others. If we believe the meat industry is responsible for serious wrongs (as I discussed in Chapter 3), then that's a good reason to say so if someone asks for our perspective on the matter. If we refused to disclose our view or tried to evade the issue, that would give others a reason to question our integrity. Yet, overtly articulating our positions is only one of many ways we can communicate our outlooks to others. The question for us here is whether failing to become vegetarian means betraying our convictions in a way that's analogous to refusing to defend them in conversation.

The value of integrity is beyond question. But we must admit some qualification to the imperative to stand up for our values, for surely the ideal of "standing for something" doesn't require expressing every conviction in every way at every opportunity. There are innumerable ways to "stand for things," and one could occupy every waking moment taking stands without exhausting the possibilities. Many ways of expressing our convictions also come with substantial costs, and there must surely be a limit to the burdens we take on to communicate our beliefs. We may grant that a person who *never* expresses her convictions likely merits criticism for failing to stand behind her values. But the fact that a person neglects to express their views along one particular dimension is very weak evidence that they're falling short of the mark.

We can bolster this point by noting that in some cases and contexts, stand-taking is positively harmful. People who never stop spouting their convictions can be intolerable, especially to those who disagree with them, and their obnoxiousness can undermine dialog and cooperation across ideological lines.[4] Certain forms of expression also put others on the defensive, making it less likely they'll engage in open-minded reflection rather than shutting down or digging in their heels. Because of considerations like these, people who hope to make genuine impacts on problems (instead of merely taking stands on them) often find it prudent to keep their cards held somewhat close to their chest.[5]

If "standing for something" is meant to serve as an ideal worthy of aspiration, it thus can't be understood as synonymous with "standing for everything that matters in all ways at all times." People of integrity will surely express their convictions in many ways. However, they'll just as surely use discretion in deciding when, how, and how much to do so. The precise details of how one should exercise this discretion elude precise formulation, as with other ideas we've discussed in this book. But any sensible way of fleshing out the picture will make room for people to choose not to engage in many actions that would express certain convictions they hold.

If this is correct, then it's once again unclear why meat-eating should be considered incompatible with adequately standing behind one's convictions. What we choose to eat *can be* a way of expressing certain views to others, and one virtue of vegetarianism is that it can play this valuable role in a person's life. But there are also countless other ways to express our convictions on this subject and others, including the conversations we make, the careers we pursue, the clothes we wear, and the actions we take as activists. Presumably, people are not obligated to orient every decision around showing others where they stand on every important issue. But if we grant this, then vegetarianism again comes out looking like one of many options for expressing oneself rather than something everyone has a specific obligation to do.

This outlook seems especially plausible when we reflect on the broader picture of responsible activism that's been unfolding over the last few chapters. According to this account, every activist faces hard decisions about how to allocate her time, energy, and resources across competing causes and projects. Responding sensibly to these choices means focusing on a few core issues rather than trying to tackle every important problem, accepting that this will mean taking little or no action on many serious problems. If we consider how a person who acts this way will look to a casual observer, we'll see their selective inaction could easily be misinterpreted as selfishness, indifference, or laziness. Such an interpretation would be mistaken, however: at best, it would be a hasty generalization from how most people tend to behave (i.e., selfishly, indifferently, and lazily); at worst, it would reflect a fundamental misunderstanding of what responsible activism looks like.

For people who allocate their efforts in the way I've described, superficial misunderstandings are likely to be a fact of life. This is likely even for those who take many steps to express their convictions in addition to their activism. Such misunderstandings seem hardly to be causes for embarrassment, however. It might be annoying when people assume that we don't care about problems we've simply chosen not to prioritize. But if we can reflect on our life as a whole and see the ways we've stood behind our convictions—including through taking constructive action—it's hard to see why we should feel ashamed when someone misconstrues something we're doing (or not doing) as a sign of unconcern.[6]

CONSUMPTION AS ENDORSEMENT

By characterizing vegetarianism as just one of many ways to express our convictions, I've implied that when a person eats meat, it's appropriate to think about this as a case of *declining an opportunity* to repudiate the meat industry. Insofar as people have innumerable opportunities to express their views, it's plausible there's nothing wrong with neglecting specific chances to do so, including by eating in a way that fails to make a statement to others. One might protest, however, that this characterization of meat-eating obscures what makes it so objectionable. By eating the meat industry's products, a critic might argue, meat-eaters don't just *neglect* to express something; they also positively express something else, namely that they *endorse* the meat industry and its practices.[7]

Even if we don't think there's a duty to take every available opportunity to express our convictions, we may still think it's wrong to express the *opposite* of what we believe. We may deny, for example, that there's a duty to plaster one's car with bumper stickers supporting causes like poverty relief and universal access to education. Yet we may still think it's wrong to display a bumper sticker reading, "KEEP EM POOR AND IGNORANT!"

It seems true that if one regards the meat industry as culpable of important misdeeds, one should avoid actions that overtly endorse its behavior. It would be problematic, for example, for a critic of the industry to voice unqualified praise of its major corporations or wear a t-shirt proudly displaying a JBS, Tyson, or Cargill logo. (There may be puzzles to untangle about ironic acts meant to express derision through superficial acts of praise, but I don't take these to contradict my general point.)

The crucial question for us is whether it's appropriate to regard meat-eating as an expression of endorsement along these lines. If we think of what most cases of meat-eating are like, this characterization hardly seems to fit. Typically, people consume meat without the thought of expressing anything to others. They want delicious, convenient, healthful, and affordable food, and they eat meat to satisfy these purely self-directed desires. Sometimes, meat-eating *does* serve an expressive purpose, but what's communicated is something other than support for the meat industry. People use meat to convey love, generosity, and many other things that have nothing to do with the issues we've been discussing.

Only rarely can the act of meat-eating be straightforwardly interpreted as a gesture of support for wrongdoing. For instance, we can imagine someone making a show of eating meat in front of vegetarians while spitefully moaning, "Mmm...animal suffering!" But although eating meat in this way seems problematic on the grounds described above, such acts are hardly representative of how most meat-eaters behave. The idea that meat-eating *as such* expresses endorsement of the meat industry's practices seems to rest on a factual mischaracterization.

THE PUZZLE OF COMPLICITY

At the beginning of this chapter, we saw Jonathan Safran Foer say that when people consume meat, they put themselves into a certain kind of relationship with the meat industry's problematic behavior. In Foer's view, we have no choice but to decide where we "hang our hats," and responsibly making that decision rules out continuing to buy and eat meat. We've seen that Foer's case looks weak if we interpret his position through the lens of expressing what we stand for. Although there's certainly a place for "hanging hats" through public expressions, the fact there are so many ways to "hang a hat" makes vegetarianism look once again like just one of many options for expressing ourselves that we have no specific duty to take up.

The issue of how we express our convictions is not the only one to arise through meat-eaters' relationship with the meat industry, however. There's also the brute fact that, by consuming the industry's products, meat-eaters participate actively in the markets which sustain the industry's objectionable behaviors. Although Chapter 4 gave us reason to doubt that any particular individual's participation *makes a difference* to what the industry does, it's nevertheless true that everyone who eats meat plays a part in facilitating the industry's continued operations.[8] Insofar as we think meat is being produced unethically, we may reasonably wonder whether this kind of connection to wrongdoing as a market participant is something people have a special obligation to avoid.

Many vegetarians cite such concerns about being implicated in wrongdoing as key motivators of their actions.[9] Even if our complicity makes no difference to what happens in the meat industry, being implicated in wrongdoing seems arguably objectionable in itself. Yet, these intuitions merit careful examination, given that all who participate in modern global civilization are personally connected to innumerable problems. The specter of global climate change, for example, is caused by everyday activities like using electricity, burning gasoline, and consuming goods and services that required energy to produce and transport. Many goods we find in stores (including many vegetables!) are produced using questionable labor practices and natural resources that were extracted in environmentally harmful ways. When we pay our taxes, we help fund and legitimize governments that commit injustices against our neighbors and others around the world. And these are just some of the *least* subtle ways in which we're entangled in injustice. Moving toward the more diffuse end of the spectrum, those of us who enjoy certain privileges in virtue of our physical features, nationality, or socioeconomic status may help perpetuate and reinforce a variety of inequities simply by living our lives.

Complexities like these are compounded by the fact that even when *we* avoid participating in market activities linked to wrongdoing, we often transact with others who use our money to engage in such activities themselves. Thus, even vegetarians can expect that some of the proceeds from the sale of vegetarian products at grocery stores and restaurants will be used to buy meat and other morally tainted products. Individuals may try to reduce these linkages by seeking out commerce with others who share their scruples. But short of establishing an entirely separate economy, "conscientious consumers" will be hard-pressed to eliminate their connections with evil completely.[10]

Reflections like these help us see that responding appropriately to complicity is not as straightforward as simply eliminating it from our lives.[11] Nor would it be desirable to *minimize* our participation to the greatest extent possible.[12] A person who quits society to live alone in the woods may achieve the cleanest hands possible, but they hardly seem like a moral exemplar worthy of emulation. Still, if *eliminating* or *minimizing* complicity are the wrong ways to respond to our connections to serious problems, what should we do instead?

The example of becoming a hermit illustrates one key dimension of this puzzle. For someone who presumably cares a great deal about the problems they've helped cause, the hermit's response is jarringly unconstructive. Going off to live in the woods is an effective way to avoid *participating* in the world's problems, but it does virtually nothing to *solve* them. The impulse to eliminate participation *as such* thus runs the risk of being objectionably self-centered. It may seem like if we really care about problems themselves, we should focus not on our personal purity but rather on more constructive ways of taking action on them.[13]

This concern becomes especially salient when we consider how tackling problems sometimes involves becoming *more* embedded in them rather than less. To cite one memorable example, when Al Gore launched his influential effort to warn of the dangers of climate change, he amassed an enormous carbon footprint traveling to speak with audiences around the world. Measured in terms of his cumulative emissions of greenhouse gases, Gore's personal contributions to causing climate change are vastly greater than yours or mine. But his contributions to *combating* climate change are also vast. Especially given that Gore's extra emissions will make no detectable difference to global climatic outcomes, it seems odd to treat his continued complicity as a serious blemish on his record of responding to this problem he's partici-pated in creating.[14]

Returning to the topic of this book, consider likewise the case of Temple Grandin, a researcher and activist who's spent her career designing slaughtering processes that reduce the chances for animals to experience suffering or fear before they're killed. Grandin's designs have been adopted through-out the meat industry, and she has become a sought-after advisor in her field.[15] Plausibly, Grandin has done more to improve the lives of meat animals than almost any other person. Yet, she has also done more than nearly anyone else to *implicate herself* in the problems that remain. As we saw in Chapter 3, Grandin's designs have by no means eliminated the meat industry's problems. Indeed, the industry's adop-tion of her suggestions has arguably helped legitimize its operations in the public eye. Moreover, Grandin openly con-tinues to eat meat—and it's plausibly instrumental to her success that she continues to do so since it's hard to imagine major meat corporations being as receptive to advice from a vegetarian. These complicity-enhancing actions notwith-standing, however, it seems strange to think of Grandin as having failed to respond adequately to the problems she's had a hand in sustaining.[16]

Plainly, most meat-eaters are not Al Gore or Temple Grandin. But these examples help highlight an important respect in

Why It's OK to Eat Meat

154

which complicity is morally puzzling. If what matters most is the problems we've helped create (as opposed to our personal purity), then it's unclear how much weight we should place on reducing complicity *as such*. We've seen that some ways of tackling problems don't involve withdrawing one's participation in helping to cause them, and many even involve *increasing* one's participation. But insofar as this is true, it's hard to see why we should focus so centrally on achieving "clean hands" rather than simply prioritizing some form of action to address the problems themselves.

The sheer number of problems in which we're implicated illuminates a second respect in which complicity is befuddling. In Chapter 4, I argued that in a problem-filled world, people face difficult decisions about which causes to focus on, in what ways, and to what extents. Even if we were to focus our attention exclusively on problems we've helped create, we'd still face a vast array of options for action. Insofar as it remains true that people will be most effective if they focus on a subset of these problems, attempting to respond to every problem in which we're implicated is the wrong ideal to pursue. Moreover, we presumably *do* want to leave room for acting on other problems (i.e., ones we haven't helped to cause) and pursuing our own projects and aspirations. In this case, the need for difficult decisions becomes even more pressing.

HOW TO RESPOND?

The preceding discussion provides several reasons for regarding complicity as a difficult thing to address appropriately. Yet, this difficulty doesn't get us off the hook for coming up with a response. As with other ideas discussed throughout this book, it seems unpromising to try to formulate a highly specific account of what this response should amount to for each of us. But there are nevertheless several broad points to make about how complicity in serious problems bears on the more general picture of responsible activism I've been developing over the last three chapters.

The first point is that there's at least some value to reducing one's complicity in wrongdoing when one can do this at a sufficiently low cost. We can see this most easily when the cost is zero. Returning to an example from the previous chapter, imagine a citizen of a smog-filled city who could eliminate their car's polluting emissions simply by pressing a button. For the sake of discussion, suppose this single car's contributions to the smog problem are so tiny that pressing this button would make no morally significant difference to the harm done by the smog. Still, the fact that pressing the button would eliminate the citizen's complicity in the problem seems like a good reason to press it.

On the other hand, the smog example also illustrates the limits of this consideration. Insofar as we grant that the car's emissions make no significant difference to the smog problem, it seems reasonable to think the citizen would be justified in declining to bear major costs to eliminate her complicity in this particular harm. This was why we concluded in the previous chapter that it might be OK for such a citizen not to install a catalytic converter when others were unlikely to do so. Especially if this citizen could think of other more constructive ways to address worldly problems through alternative efforts, it's hard to see why reducing this specific form of complicity would need to be a high priority for her. Although reducing complicity *as such* has some value, then, the forcefulness of this consideration in motivating action may nevertheless be limited in practice.

The second point to make about the significance of complicity is that it seems to provide a special reason for focusing on certain problems rather than others—one that goes beyond the more general reasons we have to tackle problems in the world. This is to say that, although we always have at least *some* reason to act in ways that help make the world a better place, the fact that certain actions help address problems we've personally helped create gives us additional reason to take those actions. Again, this is easiest to see in cases where there are no countervailing considerations. Suppose, for example, that our hypothetical car-driving citizen is deciding between two ways of becoming active in her city. One would focus on smog-fighting, and one would tackle some other issue, such as police reform, to which the citizen has no personal connection. Imagine the citizen reflects on the various merits of pursuing each form of activism and concludes they're equivalent in most respects: both tackle urgent problems; they would stand to do roughly the same amount of good in each role; both issues speak to the citizen's interests and draw well on their talents and experiences; and so on. In this apparent tie, the fact this citizen has personally contributed to the smog problem seems like a reasonable tie-breaking consideration in favor of focusing on this issue.

Once again, though, the smog example helps illustrate how limited a consideration this turns out to be. Suppose smog-fighting turned out to be a less attractive option than police reform along other dimensions—say, because the citizen would stand to do less good or prevent less harm or because they're more passionate about policing than pollution. In this case, the reason provided by the citizen's complicity would seem easily outweighed. Relatedly, the example also reinforces that *reducing* complicity is not the only way the citizen could respond to this consideration we're discussing. There are many ways to fight smog besides reducing one's personal contributions. Thus, we can grant complicity gives us reason to focus on problems we've helped create without necessarily interpreting this as a demand to reduce complicity *as such*.

One final point to make about the significance of complicity is that it suggests we ought to do more in response to the world's problems than we might otherwise consider necessary. Whatever leeway for self-development and personal enjoyment we might think ourselves entitled in a world filled with grave ills, having personally played a part in creating many of these ills gives us reason to demand more from ourselves. This is not necessarily to say we must sacrifice to the point of misery; it's just to say that we should expect people with dirty hands to contribute more toward "cleaning things up" than people whose hands are clean. Again, the example of the car-driving citizen helps us see both the significance and limits of this consideration. The fact this person is actively polluting in an ongoing way seems like a good reason to hold them to a higher standard as a problem-fighter than someone whose behaviors didn't implicate them in harm. Presumably, it would go too far to say this person should have no right to consider her own happiness and self-development while she continues driving her car. But the fact of her complicity seems like grounds for demanding at least *some* additional effort.

These points help clarify some aspects of the process for deciding how to respond conscientiously to the world's problems. This book has been intentionally vague about how we should settle which causes to tackle, in what ways, and to what extents. It has simply claimed these are difficult decisions that depend on many considerations. We can now see that some of these considerations revolve around complicity, making it attractive in several respects to focus on problems we've personally helped cause. On the other hand, we can also see these considerations aren't always—or even generally—decisive. This is especially true when it comes to demanding reductions in complicity as such. Individuals who play a role in creating problems may often continue to do so without failing ethically. This is because, even though complicity provides reasons for acting in certain ways, these reasons don't always demand reducing complicity, and there are many potentially countervailing considerations. The bottom line remains that these are complicated and multifaceted decisions. We can hardly expect every individual to prioritize any single form of activism—including ones that reduce their complicity in certain problems.

Returning to the issue of eating meat, we can see that these reflections once again undermine the case for thinking there's a general duty to become vegetarian. The fact that meat-eating implicates us in the meat industry's problems is a drawback to doing it, suggesting we should be open to vegetarian options and perhaps avoid meat when we gain nothing from eating it. The fact that meat-eaters play a role in creating these problems provides them a special reason for tackling these issues (though, as I've said, vegetarianism isn't the only option for doing this). And meat-eaters' complicity suggests they should expect more from themselves as activists than would be warranted if their hands were clean. All of these reasons help us see why vegetarianism represents one valid option for allocating one's efforts as an activist. But none is necessarily decisive. Insofar as meat-eaters *do* benefit from eating meat, insofar as they may have many reasons for focusing on different forms of activism, and insofar as they can act with appropriate ambition without becoming vegetarians, none of the arguments raised in this section yield a duty to abstain from meat. Like driving a car in a smog-filled city, eating meat doesn't prove one has failed to take seriously one's complicity in harm.

WHAT WE CELEBRATE

Pivoting from what we *express* by eating meat to how we *implicate* ourselves in the meat industry's problems doesn't yield a decisive case for vegetarianism. Yet, there's another way one might try to critique meat-eaters' relationship with meat that's worth our attention. Instead of focusing on the objective, outward features of that relationship, this line of argument focuses on how meat-eaters *feel inwardly* about the food they eat. Since meat production is linked to so many serious problems, there might seem to be something perverse about taking pleasure from meat the way meat-eaters do.

To many vegetarians, meat is a physical embodiment of cruelty, inequity, unsustainability, and recklessness. In their eyes, the only appropriate responses to meat products are negative—sadness, frustration, disgust, etc. As hard as it may be to put one's finger on what's wrong with *the act* of eating meat, it may nevertheless seem clear what's wrong with *the feelings* meat-eaters experience when they sit down to a meal. Instead of experiencing mortification before the emblems of wrongdoing on their plates, meat-eaters positively *enjoy* these foods—they celebrate meat products, seek them out, and share them with friends as if they were lovely instead of monstrous.[17] Could feelings like these be defensible?

For all the attention we tend to give to the ethics of action, it's easy to give short shrift to essentially related questions about emotion. Yet, it seems clear feelings and not just actions can be subjects of moral evaluation. For example, consider that a bigot may spend years harboring hatred in their heart without ever manifesting an outward sign to others. Although we may not be able to point to any wrongful act on the part of such an individual, we may nevertheless properly condemn their attitudes. Likewise, suppose a person responds to the death of a loving grandparent by thinking silently, "Finally—good riddance!" Even if they never show an outward sign of this attitude, the mere fact they hold it provides grounds for questioning their moral character.[18]

It seems clear there are attitudes concerning the issue of meat production that are similarly objectionable to hold. Consider, for example, how a person might react when confronted with overt cases of misconduct by meat industry employees. Many of us have witnessed graphic documentation of behaviors by industry workers so sadistic and vile they seem difficult to accept as authentic. A quick internet search will enable you to watch countless such recordings of blatant abuses against terrified and helpless animals. It seems correct to say that no one with a moral conscience could watch such acts with a happy and cheerful demeanor, and it would certainly be grotesque to respond with laughter and applause. Similar judgments seem warranted toward the other forms of wrongdoing we've discussed in this book—mistreatment of workers, environmental destruction, and the endangerment of public health. In cases like these, negative attitudes seem warranted and positive ones morally questionable.

What's at issue in these examples is our attitudes directly toward wrongful actions in the meat industry. However, many vegetarians believe similar attitudes are appropriate when faced with the products of those actions—i.e., meat. Perhaps cruelty, inequity, unsustainability, and recklessness don't "stare us in the face" in the same way when we bite into a chicken breast, pork chop, or hamburger as when we're watching disturbing videos online. But the connection between wrongdoing and meat seems relevant to what attitudes we should hold toward the latter. For example, many of us have had the experience that, after reflecting deeply on the meat industry's problems, we cannot immediately find the prospect of eating meat appetizing. But then why would it *ever* be OK to regard meat as something to be enjoyed, sought out, and even celebrated? Given what we've said in this book, can we really say such a relationship with meat amounts to anything other than denial, self-deception, or simply "looking the other way"?[19]

This line of reasoning has a powerful intuitive pull. But in what has become a recurring theme, we can see this pull begin to weaken by considering how broadly one can apply it. Searching beneath the surface tends to reveal unpleasant truths about countless aspects of our lives. The food we eat (including vegetables!), the goods we buy, the electricity that powers our lives, the civilizations we inhabit, the social relationships that structure our communities—most if not all of these things are connected to serious problems, harms, and injustices. As we attend to the badness surrounding us, we may ultimately have to ask: must we *always* feel sorrowful, guilty, and miserable? Is it *ever* OK to just set aside the problems and be happy?

These sorts of questions become especially pressing in light of our ongoing discussion of the ethics of activism. If feeling bad about a problem could drive us to solve it, that would be a powerful reason to cultivate and maintain negative attitudes. As we've seen, however, our situations as would-be activists are less glamorous. We face and are connected to countless important problems, most of which we're powerless to eliminate. We can contribute to efforts to address some of them, but it's neither obligatory nor sensible to try to tackle all of them. For a great many challenges, it seems, we'll inevitably find ourselves in the position of a passive observer. The same line of reasoning that seems to support negative feelings toward meat products thus threatens to dissatisfy us with innumerable aspects of our lives.

One natural impulse in the face of these realizations would be to ask, "What would be the *purpose* of feeling that way?" Again, we may be able to see how a certain amount of negative feeling would be valuable for motivating us to tackle the world's problems. But insofar as we accept that sensible people won't act on every problem, it may seem correspondingly pointless to sustain negative feelings in contexts where one has conscientiously decided not to focus one's efforts.

However, this line of rebuttal is incomplete because it's not true that the only reason for holding an attitude is that it serves a practical purpose. A separate virtue of an attitude is that it's *fitting to its object*: for example, there's something proper about admiring what's beautiful, fearing what's terrifying, and condemning what's wicked—and the propriety of these attitudes doesn't boil down to the practical purposes they serve.[20]

There's no doubt *something* fitting about reacting negatively to things that evoke the meat industry's problems. And insofar as fittingness can recommend an attitude without regard to its practical purpose, this seems like at least some reason for feeling negatively toward meat. Yet, the lack of connection between fittingness and practical value suggests it can be dangerous to focus too much on the former over the latter since, in some cases, holding fitting attitudes can come with practical drawbacks. When this happens, it seems appropriate to ask whether, with all things considered, the attitudes we ought to hold are the ones that are most fitting or whether it's sometimes appropriate to adopt different attitudes in deference to our other goals.[21]

We may illustrate this tension with some examples. Imagine Andy and Beth are in a romantic relationship and very much in love. Unfortunately, both are unpleasant people with rotten characters, and it's their willingness to tolerate each other's flaws that makes them such a great match. Andy and Beth try hard to work on their shortcomings, but they never seem to make much progress. So, largely as a coping mechanism, both have come to terms with their persistent failures and deficiencies. Although Andy and Beth can acknowledge that they're unsympathetic and awful in moments of reflection, they don't go about their daily lives with negative feelings about themselves and each other. On the contrary, they resolve to be cheerful, supportive, and patient, and they celebrate the good things about one another rather than dwelling on the bad.

In this example, Andy and Beth hold attitudes toward themselves and each other that are less than perfectly fitting. The attitudes that would conform most faithfully to the truth about what they're like would be negative (though perhaps with a sprinkling of compassion for their efforts to make the best of a bad situation). Yet, it seems obvious why Andy and Beth might resist holding such maximally fitting attitudes. Although practical considerations don't *exhaust* their reasons for feeling one way over another, the fact that feeling negative all the time would impede their happiness seems like a powerful consideration against sustaining such attitudes. Especially when we take the impossibility of fixing Andy's and Beth's inadequacies seriously, it seems horribly misguided to counsel these people to abandon their sunny outlooks and instead dwell painfully on the whole truth at all times.

Consider another case along similar lines. Charles lives in a city with a long history of injustice, discrimination, and corruption. Even now, social leaders and public officials in Charles' community perpetrate many harmful practices and policies that gravely impact his most vulnerable neighbors. At the same time, however, Charles' city is also a vibrant place filled with culture, tradition, and beauty. Charles recognizes he can't hope to solve all his city's problems (or many others that transcend his community's boundaries). So, in line with the discussion of the last three chapters, he sets about allocating his efforts among various causes and projects, contributing to several in ambitious ways but leaving many others unaddressed. Feeling as though he's responded appropriately to the problems surrounding him, Charles resolves to resume enjoying his city's vibrant culture, tradition, and beauty, only occasionally stopping to reflect on the many tragedies and evils that remain.

Once again, if we focus strictly on how well Charles' attitudes align with the truth about what their objects are like, we'll find a tension between how he feels most of the time and the attitudes that would be most fitting. Although the genuinely valuable aspects of Charles' community mean the most fitting attitudes wouldn't be *entirely* negative, it would nevertheless seem most fitting for him to at least feel *conflicted* about his participation in community life. Yet it once again seems clear why Charles might resist feeling conflicted when he travels about his city, participates in its culture, or chats with his neighbors around the block. Although there *are* reasons for Charles to feel conflicted, such feelings would stand to significantly impair his enjoyment of things he loves, and these burdens seem relevant to whether it makes sense for him to hold such attitudes. Insofar as Charles is doing as much to address his community's problems as he considers appropriate, it doesn't seem wrong for him to think he should be able to enjoy the other aspects of his life there without guilt. Perhaps we might expect Charles *occasionally* to feel conflicted as he reflects on his community, but it would go too far to expect him to feel that way all the time.

Following the template set by these examples helps us see why it's hard to maintain that meat-eaters go astray by enjoying their meals. Given the connections between meat and so many important problems, there's plainly *something* fitting about feeling at least some degree of negativity toward it. On the other hand, there are also typically reasons for feeling positively toward meat that one is interested in consuming (e.g., considerations of culinary merit, communion with loved ones, participation in cultural traditions). The most fitting overall attitudes toward meat would thus seemingly involve feelings that are at least conflicted, accounting for both the positive and negative aspects of the situation. However, as with countless other areas of life, sustaining conflicted emotional attitudes toward meat would be burdensome, impairing meat-eaters' ability to enjoy activities they value.

If we could justify these burdens by appealing to the need for meat-eaters to take action, say, to combat the meat industry's wrongs, that would be a good reason for sustaining them despite their costs. As I've argued throughout this book, however, there's no independent reason for thinking meat-eaters are obligated to take action in this way. If the argument for feeling conflicted is just that it's *fitting*, then the practical value of meat-eaters' own happiness would seem like a significant counterweight against the force of this consideration.

Like people who are powerless to fix every problem with their characters or the communities in which they reside, each of us must grapple with the fact that we live in a world full of serious problems we can never completely resolve. These problems permeate our lives in countless ways that are impossible to eliminate fully. I've argued in this book that the appropriate response to this state of affairs is to devote ourselves to action—for most of us, far more action than we're accustomed to taking. But I've also argued a sensible approach to activism is *selective*, focusing on certain problems and allowing many opportunities to pass by untaken.

It seems plausible that similar selectivity can be appropriately applied to emotions and not just actions, leaving us room to live our complicated lives without constantly dwelling on the badness that surrounds us. Admittedly, such an outlook won't be maximally fitting to its objects in a problem-filled world. But if we're truly working as hard as we ought to in the ways that we've chosen, is it really wrong to allow ourselves to approach the other aspects of our lives in good spirits? Would it really make us better people if we felt otherwise?

BETTER TOGETHER?

We have finally reached the end of a litany of vegetarian arguments. No doubt there are others I've neglected, but I hope the discussion has touched on the main lines of reasoning toward the claim that it's wrong to eat meat. Although each argument we've considered has sought to establish a moral duty to become vegetarian, I've tried to show that upon closer inspection, each ultimately comes up wanting. However, before declaring that it's OK to eat meat, there's one more worry that remains to consider. Even if no *single* vegetarian argument proves it's wrong to eat meat, could it still be that, when taken all together, the arguments we've been discussing yield a decisive case?

Consider in this connection the numerous virtues I've acknowledged in vegetarians' distinctive form of activism. Although no single vegetarian makes a difference to what the meat industry does, the vegetarian movement as a whole has undoubtedly had a major impact in reducing the severity of many important problems. In certain respects (e.g., through their promotion and consumption of meat alternatives), vegetarians also help build toward a world in which these problems all but disappear. Vegetarians work to pioneer norms that, if followed more broadly, would produce significant benefits. They stand publicly against the wrongdoings of meat producers, and they distance themselves personally from playing a role in those wrongs. They're able to take attitudes toward meat that are fully sensitized to the negative aspects of its production.

All of these facts represent valuable aspects of becoming a vegetarian. Even if none of these considerations is decisive on its own, there's no reason we must regard them in isolation. If one combined all the reasons for avoiding meat, it might still seem possible to assemble a definitive case for vegetarianism.

The problem with this line of reasoning is that it's in the nature of worthwhile causes that one can muster many strong reasons for promoting them. There are many ways we can make positive impacts, contribute to solving enduring wrongs, pioneer new ways of living, stand up for our values, distance ourselves from harm, and cultivate emotional attunement. As I've said throughout this book, we live in a world that's chock full of serious problems, and we have innumerable opportunities to act on them. We shouldn't be surprised to find that many candidates for our attention can give us numerous powerful reasons for selecting them.

When we consider any individual's decision about how to allocate their efforts, we must also recognize that many factors will shape their choice that resist easy generalization. Particular individuals in particular circumstances will often be distinctly well positioned to help with certain causes over others. In some cases, people may find themselves able to make an outsized impact in a certain domain because they've discovered an especially neglected project, identified a rare personal talent or skill, or simply found themselves in the right place at the right time. Some social situations may also lend themselves better to certain forms of activism over others. For example, the specific people one knows may be more susceptible to certain forms of influence, or they may represent valuable connections one can use in particular ways. A person's distinctive blend of interests, passions, experiences, and personality traits may guide them toward certain causes as well. When a person finds certain forms of action positively enjoyable, beneficial, or easy, they may be able to devote themselves to those activities with great enthusiasm without unduly exhausting their limited bandwidth for activism. To decide which causes to support, in what ways, and to what extents, one must consider all these factors. It simply seems false that vegetarianism will always emerge from that decision-making process as one of the winning candidates.

As we decide how to answer the call of the world's many problems, we should expect that what counts as the best form of activism for us will likely be different from what's best for others. In this respect, the choice of activist pursuits will be similar to the choice of a career. No doubt some options are better than others in both of these domains, but no single option is best for everybody. Vegetarianism seems no different from countless other forms of activism in this respect.

For some people, the considerations we've discussed in vegetarianism's favor may make it a no-brainer. This is especially likely for those who are happily practicing vegetarianism already, have gone through the frictions of adapting their lifestyles to this diet, are knowledgeable about the issues we've discussed, and identify strongly with this particular form of activism. On the other hand, other people may find vegetarianism a distinctly repellent way to tackle the world's problems—or at least a less compelling option than others that are available. We cannot diagnose a moral failure in people like these just because they've omitted to take up this one specific form of activism.

IT'S OK TO EAT MEAT

Thus, we finally arrive at the conclusion I have been working to establish in this book. It's OK to eat meat, and not just the meticulously produced offerings at farmer's markets and farm-to-table restaurants. It's OK to eat meat produced in morally dubious ways—and it's OK to do so while condemning the wrongdoing that resulted in its creation. It's OK to eat meat, not just when it's necessary or on rare special occasions, but "in the regular way" that involves making it a standard part of one's supermarket purchases and restaurant orders and eating it simply because one wants it.

There are, as we've seen, ethical downsides to behaviors like these. There are likewise ethical downsides to countless other activities that make up our complicated lives in our imperfect world. Correspondingly, one can marshall numerous considerations on behalf of avoiding meat. But these considerations can be multiplied in countless ways as well, recommending a wide range of actions to respond to the world's many problems. Not only is there no obligation to avoid every action with downsides like these or to take up every cause with corresponding upsides: I've argued it would be unwise to try to accomplish such a feat. If we really care about responding sensibly to the innumerable ills that surround us, we'll confront the difficult task of *deciding* which problems to tackle, how, and how much; and we'll accept that once we've carried out our intentions, our efforts will leave a great many problems unaddressed—potentially including those we've discussed in this book.

At this point, I hope you'll agree that it's OK to eat meat. However, I also hope that's not the main thing you'll take from this book. As you must surely realize, the real punch line here isn't simply about the *moral right to decline* to become vegetarian; it's also about the *moral right to do something else instead*. In a highly imperfect world like ours, each of us has a moral duty to pitch in somehow to help make things better. Vegetarianism fails to stand out as a single thing that's required of us mainly because there are so many other options. However, the fact remains that most meat-eaters aren't doing what they're doing because they're exercising this latitude to prioritize other forms of action. They eat the way they do as one of many manifestations of their laziness, selfishness, and indifference. Many vegetarians, too, are guilty of laziness, selfishness, and indifference as they fool themselves into thinking that their ineffectual dietary choices are enough for a clear conscience in our problem-filled world. If you're a meat-eater or a vegetarian who merits such a description, I hope you'll agree with me in saying *that* is not OK. You should be doing more; it's just up to you to decide how.

So, then, it's now up to you. *What else will you do?*

Notes

IS IT OK TO EAT MEAT?

1 For discussion of trends in vegetarianism in the US context—and some of the difficulties in measuring them accurately—see Saulius Šimčikas, "Is the Percentage of Vegetarians and Vegans in the U.S. Increasing?" *Animal Charity Evaluators* (2018), available online at https://animalcharityevaluators.org/blog/is-the-percentage-of-vegetarians-and-vegans-in-the-u-s-increasing/.

2 One other terminological point: as we'll discuss in later chapters, new technological advancements are beginning to make it possible to produce "meat"—i.e., animal muscle tissues—without raising and killing animals. In this book, when I talk about "meat," I'll be talking about the kind of meat that comes from killing animals rather than tissues synthesized or grown in a lab.

3 Hannah Ritchie and Max Roser, "Meat and Dairy Production," *Our World in Data* (2019), available online at https://ourworldindata.org/meat-production.

4 Humane Research Council, "Study of Current and Former Vegetarians and Vegans" (2014), available online at https://faunalytics.org/wp-content/uploads/2015/06/Faunalytics_Current-Former-Vegetarians_Full-Report.pdf. This underestimates the true extent of reversion since at least some survey participants who are currently experimenting with vegetarianism will go back to eating meat as well. Of those who had given up vegetarianism in the study, about a third reverted within three months; more than half did so within a year; and more than two-thirds did within two years. Among the currently vegetarian participants, 5% had adhered to their diets for less than three months, 13% for less than a year, and 20% for less than two years.

5 In this connection, many vegetarians were once meat-eaters, and they often invoke explanations like these to account for their former behavior. See, e.g., Michael Huemer, *Dialogues on Ethical Vegetarianism* (New York: Routledge, 2019), xii–xiv.

6 See along these lines Loren Lomasky, "Is It Wrong to Eat Animals?" *Social Philosophy & Policy* 30, nos. 1–2 (2013): 177–200.

7 It's not clear this argument would be decisive even if we were willing to grant it. Suppose it turned out that, due to a bizarre feature of human psychology, owning slaves makes people substantially happier than it's possible to be without slaves. At most, this would show there's something tragic about how humans are built that makes it impossible to be fully happy while also living ethically.

8 See, e.g., Yotam Ottolenghi, *Plenty* (San Francisco: Chronicle Books, 2011).

9 See on this point Peter Singer, *Animal Liberation, Updated Edition* (New York: HarperCollins, [1975] 1999), 178.

10 See, e.g., Tamara M. Pfeiler and Boris Egloff, "Do Vegetarians Feel Bad? Examining the Association between Eating Vegetarian and Subjective Well-Being in Two Representative Samples," *Food Quality and Preference* 86 (2020), article 104018.

11 See, e.g., Jonathan Safran Foer, *Eating Animals* (New York: Little, Brown & Co., 2009), chs. 1 and 8.

12 See, e.g., H.K. Biesalski, "Meat as a Component of a Healthy Diet—Are There Any Risks or Benefits if Meat Is Avoided in the Diet?" *Meat Science* 70, no. 3 (2005): 509–524; PaleoLeap, "How Vegetarianism Is Bad For You and the Environment," *PaleoLeap* (2020), available online at https://paleoleap.com/vegetarianism-bad-environment/.

13 See, e.g., Mayo Clinic Staff, "Vegetarian Diet: How to Get the Best Nutrition," *Healthy Lifestyle: Nutrition and Healthy Eating* (2020), available online at https://www.mayoclinic.org/healthy-lifestyle/nutrition-and-healthy-eating/in-depth/vegetarian-diet/art-20046446.

14 See, e.g., A. Wolk, "Potential Health Hazards of Eating Red Meat," *Journal of Internal Medicine* 281, no. 2 (2017): 106–122.

15 Some proponents of meat-eating acknowledge it only takes a tiny amount to achieve the distinctive fulfillments associated with the practice, and they conclude on this basis that people should drastically reduce their consumption of meat. For example, Dominique Lestel, in *Eat This Book: A Carnivore's Manifesto* (New York: Columbia University Press, 2016), insists people have an *ethical duty* to eat meat as a way of spiritually internalizing their nature as animals. Yet, he grants that "Factory farming is a disgrace" and "In rich countries, the consumption of meat has become a habit that no longer involves a hint of commemoration or communion" (77). Hence Lestel insists we eat *some* meat but agrees people should drastically reduce their consumption. As my preceding comments indicate, I don't find plausible Lestel's views regarding an alleged duty to eat meat (or the claims about "animality" on which he bases them). For present purposes, however, the more important difference between us has to do with my aim to defend eating meat "in the regular way" and not only as merely a ceremonial indulgence.

16 See, e.g., Jeffrey Kluger, "Sorry Vegans: Here's How Meat-Eating Made Us Human," TIME (2016), available online at https://time.com/4252373/meat-eating-veganism-evolution/.

17 I should note, however, that there are examples of meat-eaters advancing arguments in this vein. See, e.g., Christopher Belshaw, "Meat," in The Moral Complexities of Eating Meat, edited by Ben Bramble and Bob Fischer (New York: Oxford University Press, 2016), 9–29, at 20.

18 For a classic treatment of this point, see John Stuart Mill, "On Nature," in Nature, the Utility of Religion, and Theism (London: Longmans, Green & Co., [1874] 1885), 3–65.

19 For discussion of the decline in violence in recent human history, see Steven Pinker, The Better Angels of Our Nature: Why Violence Has Declined (New York: Viking Books, 2011).

20 See, e.g., Plato, "Gorgias," in Plato: Complete Works, edited by John M. Cooper (Indianapolis, IN: Hackett Publishing Co., 1997), 791–869, at 827–828.

21 Genesis 9:2–3 (NRSV).

22 Genesis 1:29.

23 Genesis 9:3.

24 Leviticus 11.

25 Isaiah 11:6–9.

26 Isaiah 66:3.

27 E.g., Exodus 21:1–27; Leviticus 25:39–46.

28 Exodus 21:20–21.

29 Leviticus 20:9–10.

30 Leviticus 20:13.

31 We can find examples of this strategy particularly within Christian traditions. In Romans, Paul insists that Gentiles should not fixate on the details of Jewish law since, for them, salvation is fundamentally about faith in God rather than compliance with a particular code of conduct. Along similar lines, the Catechism of the Catholic Church 577–582, available online at https://www.vatican.va/archive/ENG0015/__P1N.htm, contends Jesus fulfilled the Jewish law and brought about the redemption of acts that transgress against it.

32 See, e.g., Philo of Alexandria, Philo in Ten Volumes, and Two Supplementary Volumes (Cambridge, MA: Harvard University Press, 1929–1962); Origen, On First Principles (New York: Harper & Row, 1966); Saint Augustine, On Genesis, translated by Edmund Hill and edited by John E. Rotelle (New City Press, 2002).

33 Mark 7:18–21.

34 1 Corinthians 10:31.

35 1 Corinthians 10:23.

36 For attempts to develop such an argument, see Andrew Linzey, Animal Theology (Urbana, IL: University of Illinois Press, 1994); Matthew Scully, Dominion: The Power of Man, the Suffering of Animals, and the Call to Mercy (New York: St. Martin's Press, 2002).

37 See, e.g., Jeremy R. Garrett, "Utilitarianism, Vegetarianism, and Human Health: A Response to the Causal Impotence Objection," *Journal of Applied Philosophy* 24, no. 3 (2007): 223–237. For a prominent example of the sort of health study invoked to defend this view, see T. Colin Campbell and Thomas M. Campbell II, *The China Study, Revised and Expanded Edition* (Dallas: BenBella Books, 2016).

38 E.g., Mayo Clinic Staff, "How Meat and Poultry Fit In Your Healthy Diet," *Healthy Lifestyle: Nutrition and Healthy Eating* (2019), available online at https://www.mayoclinic.org/healthy-lifestyle/nutrition-and-healthy-eating/in-depth/food-and-nutrition/art-20048095.

39 This claim does not depend on the thesis that small amounts of meat are completely safe. Even if there turns out to be some risk associated with consuming even tiny quantities of meat, it would not be absurd for someone to regard these risks as worthwhile for the sake of the benefits of eating meat. Consider in this connection that every time you get into a car, you increase your chances of death or permanent disability, and yet most of us don't regard this as a decisive reason never to get into a car. On the other hand, some people may find it easier to maintain a healthy diet by avoiding all meat, perhaps because they're prone to "overdo it" when they allow themselves to have any. These people may have good practical reasons to become vegetarians, but this would not imply a moral duty to do so in any broader sense. Consider in this connection that some recovering alcoholics find it easiest to maintain control if they abstain from drinking entirely, but this doesn't imply the rest of us are obligated to do the same.

40 For reservations about this view, see Christine Korsgaard, *Fellow Creatures: Our Obligations to the Other Animals* (New York: Oxford University Press, 2018), 221.

41 This strategy runs the risk of ignoring potential synergies among different vegetarian arguments. I take up this possibility in Chapter 6.

42 It's worth clarifying that proponents of "wrong in principle" arguments aren't necessarily committed to claiming that eating meat is wrong *no matter what*. If the planet's survival depended on eating a bite of meat, I take it that virtually every vegetarian would do it. By the same token, if the planet's survival depended on capturing another human being to be your slave, I bet you would do it. Yet, this doesn't undermine the claim that slavery is wrong as a matter of principle. It just shows that even powerful moral principles can sometimes give way in the face of extreme situations.

43 See, e.g., Michael Pollan, *The Omnivore's Dilemma: A Natural History of Four Meals* (New York: Penguin Books, 2006); Terence Cuneo, "Conscientious Omnivorism," in *Philosophy Comes to Dinner: Arguments about the Ethics of Eating*, edited by Andrew Chignell, Terence Cuneo, and Matthew C. Halteman (New York: Routledge, 2016), 21–38.

44 David DeGrazia, "Moral Vegetarianism from a Very Broad Base," *Journal of Moral Philosophy* 6, no. 2 (2009): 143–165, at 157.

CONSCIENTIOUS OMNIVORISM

1 Tom Regan, *The Case for Animal Rights* (Berkeley, CA: University of California Press, 1987), 344.

2 In this connection, the vegetarian author David DeGrazia, in "Moral Vegetarianism from a Very Broad Basis," *Journal of Moral Philosophy* 6, no. 2 (2009): 143–165, argues his compatriots do their cause a disservice by focusing so much on the controversial moral outlooks discussed in this chapter since even a moderate level of concern for animals is enough to illuminate the moral problems with mainstream meat production.

3 See, e.g., Peter Singer, "All Animals are Equal," *Philosophic Exchange* 5, no. 1 (1974): 103–116; Regan, *The Case for Animal Rights*, 151–156, 279–280; Gary Francione, *Introduction to Animal Rights:Your Child or the Dog* (Philadelphia: Temple University Press, 2000), 111–129; Daniel A. Dombrowski, *Babies and Beasts:The Argument from Marginal Cases* (Urbana, IL: University of Illinois Press, 1997); Alistair Norcross, "Puppies, Pigs, and People: Eating Meat and Marginal Cases," *Philosophical Perspectives* 18 (2004): 229–245; Oscar Horta, "The Scope of the Argument from Species Overlap," *Journal of Applied Philosophy* 31, no. 2 (2014): 142–154; Michael Huemer, *Dialogues on Ethical Vegetarianism* (New York: Routledge, 2019), 15–16.

4 Singer, "All Animals are Equal," 111; see also Singer, *Animal Liberation*, 19–20; Regan, *The Case for Animal Rights*, 151–156.

5 Peter Singer, *Animal Liberation, Updated Edition* (New York: HarperCollins, 2009), 230.

6 E.g., Eva Feder Kittay, "The Personal Is Philosophical Is Political: A Philosopher and Mother of a Cognitively Disabled Person Sends Notes from the Battlefield," *Metaphilosophy* 40, nos. 3–4 (2009): 606–627.

7 For elaboration on how Singer thinks we may account for severely cognitively disabled infants in moral deliberation, see Peter Singer, *Practical Ethics,Third Edition* (New York: Cambridge University Press, 2011), 160–167.

8 E.g., Regan, *The Case for Animal Rights*, 218–221; Francione, *Introduction to Animal Rights*, ch. 6.

9 For further discussion, see Christine Korsgaard, *Fellow Creatures: Our Obligations to the Other Animals* (New York: Oxford University Press, 2018), 5–8.

10 As Tom Regan acknowledges in *The Case for Animal Rights*, 246, the explanation provided by such accounts is actually not fully adequate since they cannot straightforwardly account for our attitudes toward humans who are not sentient and cannot experience their lives—including dead ones. I will take up this problem in greater depth below.

11 In the context of debates over eating meat, arguments like these have been linked especially to "contractarian" theories of morality. See, e.g., Peter Carruthers, *The Animals Issue* (New York: Cambridge University Press, 1992). However, I take it the ideas sketched here encompass not only contractarian paradigms but also other canonical perspectives from, e.g., Plato, Aristotle, Hume, Bentham, Kant, and Mill. For an overview of classic ethical theories from a variety of traditions, see Russ Shafer-Landau, *Living Ethics: An Introduction with Readings* (New York: Oxford University Press, 2019).

12 John Rawls, *A Theory of Justice, Revised Edition* (Cambridge, MA: Harvard University Press, 1999), §77; Bernard Williams, "The Human Prejudice," in *Philosophy as a Humanistic Discipline* (Princeton, N.J.: Princeton University Press, 2006), 135–152; Douglas MacLean, "Is 'Human Being' a Moral Concept?" *Philosophy & Public Policy Quarterly* 30, nos. 3–4 (2010): 16–20. Along similar lines, Loren Lomasky, in *Persons, Rights, and the Moral Community* (New York: Oxford University Press, 1987), 204–205 and 223, argues social practices are inevitably designed to appeal to "classes" of beings (e.g., "children," "humans," or "mankind"), such that the regard we show for severely cognitively disabled humans effectively "piggybacks on those who are unimpaired" (ibid., 205).

13 On the origins of the term "speciesism," see Richard Ryder, "Speciesism Again: The Original Leaflet," *Critical Society* 2 (2010).

14 E.g., Norcross, "Puppies, Pigs, and People."

15 Hilde Lindemann Nelson, "What Child Is This?" *Hastings Center Report* 32, no. 6 (2002): 29–38; Elizabeth Anderson, "Animal Rights and the Values of Nonhuman Life," in *Animal Rights: Current Debates and New Directions*, edited by Cass R. Sunstein and Martha Nussbaum (New York: Oxford University Press, 2004), 277–298.

16 See, e.g., Norcross, "Puppies, Pigs, and People."

17 For favorable consideration of this possibility, see Raymond G. Frey, "Moral Standing, the Value of Lives, and Speciesism," *Between the Species* 4, no. 3 (1988): 191–201.

18 Cora Diamond, "Eating Animals and Eating People," *Philosophy* 53, no. 20 (1978): 465–479.

19 Ibid., 467, emphasis original.

20 In the literature on the ethics of eating meat, a curious debate has emerged over the ethics of eating roadkill. See on this issue Donald W. Bruckner, "Strict Vegetarianism is Immoral," in *The Moral Complexities of Eating Meat*, edited by Ben Bramble and Bob Fischer (New York: Oxford University Press, 2016), 30–47; Cheryl Abbate, "Save the Meat for Cats: Why It's Wrong to Eat Roadkill," *Journal of Agricultural and Environmental Ethics* 32, no. 1 (2019): 165–182; Bob Fischer, *The Ethics of Eating Meat: Usually Bad, Sometimes Wrong, Often Permissible* (New York: Routledge, 2020), 110–112.

21 For endorsement of Diamond's view, however, see Lori Gruen, *Ethics and Animals: An Introduction* (New York: Cambridge University Press, 2011), 101–104.

22 The concept of "dignity" is often linked to Kant's ethics and the idea of treating something as an inviolable "end in itself." In this section, I don't want to take a precise position on what "dignity" amounts to. Rather, I'll simply use the term as a stand-in for whatever it is about other people that makes us consider it disrespectful to consume their flesh regardless of how it was procured.

23 See on this point Bob Fischer, *The Ethics of Eating Animals: Usually Bad, Sometimes Wrong, Often Permissible* (New York: Routledge, 2020), 100–101.

24 For an answer in the affirmative, see Christine Korsgaard, in *Fellow Creatures*, 221.

25 E.g., Ty Raterman, "An Environmentalist's Lament of Predation," *Environmental Ethics* 30, no. 4 (2008): 417–434; Jeff McMahan, "The Moral Problem of Predation," in Andrew Chignell, Terence Cuneo, Matthew C. Halteman, *Philosophy Comes to Dinner: Arguments about the Ethics of Eating* (New York: Routledge, 2016), 268–293. For discussion of these views, see Jennifer Everett, "Environmental Ethics, Animal Welfarism, and the Problem of Predation: A Bambi Lover's Respect for Nature," *Ethics & the Environment* 6, no. 1 (2001): 42–67; Clare Palmer, *Animal Ethics in Context* (New York: Columbia University Press, 2010).

26 E.g., J. Baird Callicott, "Animal Liberation: A Triangular Affair," *Environmental Ethics* 2, no. 4 (1980): 311–338; Mark Sagoff, "Animal Liberation and Environmental Ethics: Bad Marriage, Quick Divorce," *Osgoode Hall Law Journal* 22, no. 2 (1984): 297–307.

27 Val Plumwood, "Being Prey," *Terra Nova* 1, no. 3 (1996): 32–44. See along similar lines Dominique Lestel, *Eat This Book: A Carnivore's Manifesto* (New York: Columbia University Press, 2016).

28 Jeff McMahan, *The Ethics of Killing*, 194–203. Similar arguments have been presented by other vegetarian authors, including David DeGrazia, "Moral Vegetarianism from a Very Broad Basis," 161–164; Tristram McPherson, "Why I Am a Vegan (and You Should Be One Too)," in *Philosophy Comes to Dinner: Arguments about the Ethics of Eating*, edited by Andrew Chignell, Terence Cuneo, and Matthew C. Halteman (New York: Routledge, 2016), 73–91, at 77–80.

29 In contrast, some authors have argued that we must transform our outlook towards animals because their cognitive abilities are much more advanced than was historically understood. To cite just one example, Duncan Purves and Nicolas Delon, in "Meaning in the Lives of Humans and Other Animals," *Philosophical Studies* 175, no. 2 (2018): 317–338, argue that animals' lives may contain much more meaning than has traditionally been assumed. The true details of animals' cognitive lives continue to be debated on both scientific and conceptual grounds, and

I don't want to try to settle these controversies in this book. Instead, I'll simply note that the more sophisticated animal cognition actually turns out to be, the more reason you'll have to re-examine the arguments I put forward in this chapter and consider whether they can be sustained in the face of this greater level of sophistication. In this connection, I think it's quite plausible to say we should not farm and eat chimpanzees, dolphins, and elephants as a matter of principle—regardless of how they're treated in the process—because these beings have reached a level of cognitive sophistication that entitles them to genuine respect.

30 For reservations about this concession, see Loren Lomasky, "Is It Wrong to Eat Animals?" *Social Philosophy & Policy* 30, nos. 1–2 (2013): 177–200.

31 E.g., Christopher Belshaw, "Meat," in *The Moral Complexities of Eating Meat*, edited by Ben Bramble and Bob Fischer (New York: Oxford University Press, 2016), 9–29, at 21–24.

32 Jeff McMahan, "Eating Animals the Nice Way," *Dædalus* 137, no. 1 (2008): 66–76, at 67–68.

33 Ibid., 73.

34 Ibid.

35 For one discussion of the importance of such justifications, see John Rawls, "Two Concepts of Rules," *The Philosophical Review* 64, no. 1 (1955): 3–32.

36 For his part, McMahan defends his ambitious thesis with only a single illustration:

> Suppose that we could permissibly program an automatic nuclear retaliatory device to annihilate an enemy country if it strikes us first, provided that programming the device would have a high probability of deterring a nuclear first strike that would otherwise be highly probable. We could also permissibly *threaten* a country with retaliatory annihilation to deter a nuclear first strike. But if this threat were to fail and the enemy country were to launch a first strike, it could not possibly be permissible at that point to fulfill our threat by annihilating the enemy country when doing so would serve no purpose whatsoever
>
> (McMahan, "Eating Animals the Nice Way," 73).

It is on the strength of this example that McMahan concludes that we must evaluate individual on their individual merits and not by appeal to the practices in which they are embedded (ibid). However, it seems clear McMahan has misinterpreted the significance of this specific example. The case of nuclear retaliation illustrates a special problem for practices of *deterrence*, not a problem with appealing to practices more generally. The difficulty with deterrence is that it typically involves threatening to do something terrible for *the specific purpose of preventing something bad from happening.* The result of this is that once we are in a position to carry through with our threat, it will necessarily be the case that our preventative efforts have failed. Whether we can justify practices of deterrence despite this fact is unimportant for our purposes. The more important point is that whatever reservations McMahan may have about the legitimacy of deterrence, this does not provide a compelling reason to doubt the legitimacy of practice-based justifications more generally.

37 Ibid., 73–74.
38 McMahan does not specifically present this example, but he discusses and endorses several analogous examples of "programming a device" to carry out multi-step tasks that he considers impermissible for humans to perform in ibid., 73.
39 Ibid., 69, 74–75.
40 McMahan, *The Ethics of Killing*, 207.
41 Stated more carefully: this is what it would take to show it's *conceptually impossible* to eat meat conscientiously. A different way to attack conscientious omnivorism would be to argue that, as a practical matter, there's something *inherently unworkable* about what conscientious omnivores propose. Peter Singer attempts an argument like this in *Animal Liberation*, claiming that allowing oneself to eat the most sensitively raised animals will inevitably send one down a slippery slope to all kinds of meat-eating:

> As a matter of strict logic, perhaps, there is no contradiction in taking an interest in animals on both compassionate and gastronomic grounds. If one is opposed to inflicting suffering on animals, but not to the painless killing of animals, one could consistently eat animals who had lived free of all suffering and been instantly, painlessly slaughtered. Yet practically and psychologically it is impossible to be consistent in one's concern for nonhuman animals while continuing to dine on them. If we are prepared to take the life of another being merely in order to satisfy our taste for a particular type of food, then that being is no more than a means to our end. In time we will come to regard pigs, cattle, and chickens as things for our use, no matter how strong our compassion may be; and when we find that to continue to obtain supplies of the bodies of these animals at a price we are able to pay it is necessary to change their living conditions a little, we will be unlikely to regard these changes too critically. The factory farm is nothing more than the application of technology to the idea that animals are means to our ends (160–161).

This line of reasoning seems dubious in much the same way as the view that it's impossible to drink alcohol responsibly since any attempt to do so will inevitably lead to liquor store holdups the moment one's budget gets tight. However, since this book's ultimate goal is to show that even "conscientious omnivores" are mistaken about the ethics of eating meat, I will not dwell further on the matter of defending their position against arguments like Singer's.

THE OTHER 99%

1 Peter Singer, *Animal Liberation, Updated Edition* (New York: HarperCollins, 1999), 160; Michael Huemer, *Dialogues on Ethical Vegetarianism* (New York: Routledge, 2019), 25.

2 One other important constraint on this chapter's focus has to do with this book's focus on *consumer* ethics. Despite the many concerns and criticisms I'll raise about the meat industry in this chapter, I'll have frustratingly little to say about how best to make things better in the industry or how individual industry participants should respond to the worries I raise. For some efforts to begin theorizing about these important matters, see G. John Benson and Bernard E. Rollin, *The Well-being of Farm Animals: Challenges and Solutions* (Ames, IA: Blackwell, 2004); Paul B. Thompson, "Philosophical Ethics and the Improvement of Farmed Animal Lives," *Animal Frontiers* 10, no. 1 (2020): 21–28.

3 Philip Clauer, "Modern Meat Chicken Industry," *Penn State Extension* (2012), available online at https://extension.psu.edu/modern-meat-chicken-industry.

4 National Chicken Council, "Processing: How Are Chickens Slaughtered and Processed for Meat?" *Chicken Check In* (2021), available online at https://www.chickencheck.in/faq/how-chickens-slaughtered-processed/.

5 Of particular note is my omission of discussion of breeding hens— i.e., the chickens that lay the eggs that eventually become broiler chicks. For discussion of some of the very different issues that arise with these breeding hens, see I.C. de Jong and D. Guémené, "Major Welfare Issues in Broiler Breeders," *World's Poultry Science Journal* 67, no. 1 (2011): 73–82.

6 EFSA Panel on Animal Health and Welfare, "Killing for Purposes Other than Slaughter: Poultry," *EFSA Journal* 17, no. 11, art. 5850 (2019), 17.

7 Ibid., 32–33, 59. Culling is sometimes done by suffocating chicks with carbon dioxide, nitrogen, or some other gas (ibid., 29–30). These methods come with welfare concerns of their own (ibid., 73; B.I. Baker, S. Torrey, T.M. Widowski, P.V. Turner, T.D. Knezacek, J. Nicholds, T.G. Crowe, K. Schwean-Lardner, "Evaluation of Carbon Dioxide Induction Methods for the Euthanasia of Day-Old Cull Broiler Chicks," *Poultry Science* 98, no. 5 (2019): 2043–2053.)

8 The Humane Society of the United States, "Welfare Issues with the Transport of Day-Old Chicks" (2008), available online at https://www.humanesociety.org/sites/default/files/docs/hsus-report-chick-transport-welfiss.pdf; EFSA Panel on Animal Health and Welfare, "Scientific Opinion Concerning the Welfare of Animals during Transport," *EFSA Journal* 9, no. 1, art. 1966 (2011), 49–52.

9 A. Al Homidan, J.F. Robertson, and A.M. Petchey, "Review of the Effect of Ammonia and Dust Concentrations on Broiler Performance," *World's Poultry Science Journal* 59, no. 3 (2003): 340–349; W. Bessei, "Welfare of Broilers: A Review," *World's Poultry Science Journal* 62, no. 3 (2006): 455–466, at 458–459.

10 Michael D. Ruff, "Important Parasites in Poultry Production Systems," *Veterinary Parasitology* 84, nos. 3–4 (1999): 337–347.

11 Bessei, "Welfare of Broilers," 456–458.

12 Ibid., 461–462.

13 C.J. Nicol and G.B. Scott, "Pre-slaughter Handling and Transport of Broiler Chickens," *Applied Animal Behaviour Science* 28, nos. 1–2 (1990): 57–73; Leonie Jacobs, Evelyn Delezie, Luc Duchateau, Klara Goethals, and Frank A.M. Tuyttens, "Impact of the Separate Pre-slaughter Stages on Broiler Chicken Welfare," *Poultry Science* 96, no. 2 (2017): 266–273.

14 EFSA Panel on Animal Health and Welfare, "Slaughter of Animals: Poultry," *EFSA Journal* 17, no. 11, art. 5849 (2019), 40–44.

15 Ibid., 58.

16 Ibid., 50.

17 National Chicken Council, "U.S. Broiler Performance: 1925 to Present" (2021), available online at https://www.nationalchickencouncil.org/statistic/us-broiler-performance/.

18 National Chicken Council, "Broiler Chicken Industry Key Facts 2020" (2021), available online at https://www.nationalchickencouncil.org/statistic/broiler-industry-key-facts/.

19 Ibid.

20 James M. MacDonald, *Technology, Organization, and Financial Performance in U.S. Broiler Production* (Washington, DC: U.S. Department of Agriculture Economic Research Service, 2014), 42.

21 Ibid., 15.

22 Ibid., 15–17.

23 Ibid., 26–29.

24 SalaryExpert, "Chicken Catcher Salary" (2021), available online at https://www.salaryexpert.com/salary/job/chicken-catcher/united-states; SalaryExpert, "Slaughter Laborer" (2021), available online at https://www.salaryexpert.com/salary/job/slaughter-laborer/united-states.

25 Steven W. Lenhart, Peter D. Morris, Robert E. Akin, Stephen A. Olenchock, William S. Service, and William P. Boone, "Organic Dust, Endotoxin,

and Ammonia Exposures in the North Carolina Poultry Processing Industry," *Applied Occupational and Environmental Hygiene* 5, no. 9 (1990): 611–618; Kelley J. Donham, Debra Cumro, and Steve Reynolds, "Synergistic Effects of Dust and Ammonia on the Occupational Health Effects of Poultry Production Worlers," *Journal of Agromedicine* 8, no. 2 (2002): 57–76; Ioannis Basinas, Torben Sigsgaard, Hans Kromhout, Dick Heederik, Inge M. Wouters, and Vivi Schlünssen, "A Comprehensive Review of Levels and Determinants of Personal Exposure to Dust and Endotoxin in Livestock Farming," *Journal of Exposure Science and Environmental Epidemiology* 25, no. 2 (2015): 123–137.

26 Human Rights Watch, *"When We're Dead and Buried, Our Bones Will Keep Hurting": Workers' Rights Under Threat in US Meat and Poultry Plants* (New York: Human Rights Watch, 2019), 33–39.

27 Ibid., 49–74.

28 Centers for Disease Control, "COVID-19 Among Workers in Meat and Poultry Processing Facilities—United States, April–May 2020," *Morbidity and Mortality Weekly Report* 69, no. 27 (2020): 887–892.

29 Human Rights Watch, *"When We're Dead and Buried,"* 44–48.

30 Ibid., 18–22.

31 Human Rights Watch, *Blood, Sweat, and Fear: Workers' Rights in U.S. Meat and Poultry Plants* (New York: Human Rights Watch, 2004), ch. 6.

32 U.S. Environmental Protection Agency, "Estimated Animal Agriculture Nitrogen and Phosphorus from Manure" (2021), available online at https://www.epa.gov/nutrient-policy-data/estimated-animal-agriculture-nitrogen-and-phosphorus-manure.

33 Dan L. Cunningham, "Nuisance Myths and Poultry Farming," *Learning for Life Bulletin* 1299 (Athens, GA: University of Georgia Extension, 2012).

34 E.g., Jonathan Safran Foer, *Eating Animals* (New York: Little, Brown & Co., 2009), ch. 5; Jonathan Anomaly, "What's Wrong with Factory Farming?" *Public Health Ethics* 8, no. 3 (2015): 246–254.

35 U.S. Environmental Protection Agency, "National Pollutant Discharge Elimination System (NPDES): Animal Feeding Operations (AFOs)," (2020), available online at https://www.epa.gov/npdes/animal-feeding-operations-afos.

36 U.S. Environmental Protection Agency, "National Air Emissions Monitoring Study" (2020), available online at https://www.epa.gov/afos-air/national-air-emissions-monitoring-study.

37 U.S. Department of Agriculture, "Defend the Flock Program" (2021), available online at https://www.aphis.usda.gov/aphis/ourfocus/animalhealth/animal-disease-information/avian/defend-the-flock-program.

38 National Chicken Council, "Questions and Answers about Antibiotics in Chicken Production" (2019), available online at https://www.nationalchickencouncil.org/questions-answers-antibiotics-chicken-production/.

39 E.g., Tyson Foods, "Environment: Summary Overview" (2020), available online at https://www.tysonsustainability.com/environment/; Pilgrim's Pride, "Environment" (2020), available online at https://sustainability.pilgrims.com/chapters/environment/.

40 William D. McBride and Nigel Key, *US Hog Production from 1992 to 2009: Technology, Restructuring, and Productivity Growth* (Washington, DC: U.S. Department of Agriculture, 2013).

41 Jeremy N. Marchant-Forde, *Sow Welfare Fact Sheet: Housing and Welfare of Sows during Gestation* (West Lafayette, IN: USDA Agricultural Research Service, 2010); American Veterinary Medical Association, "Welfare Implications of Gestation Sow Housing" (2015), available online at https://www.avma.org/resources-tools/literature-reviews/welfare-implications-gestation-sow-housing.

42 Jeremy N. Marchant-Forde, *Swine Welfare Fact Sheet: Welfare of Sows and Piglets at Farrowing* (West Lafayette, IN: USDA Agricultural Research Service, 2011).

43 Pork Checkoff, "Life Cycle of a Market Pig" (2016), available online at https://www.pork.org/facts/pig-farming/life-cycle-of-a-market-pig/.

44 For a video presentation of the slaughtering process as viewed through the eyes of the industry, see North American Meat Institute, "Video Tour of a Pork Plant featuring Temple Grandin" (2013), available online at https://www.youtube.com/watch?v=LsEbvwMipJI.

45 Jeremy N. Marchant-Forde, *Sow Welfare Fact Sheet: Housing and Welfare of Sows during Gestation* (West Lafayette, IN: USDA Agricultural Research Service, 2010); American Veterinary Medical Association, "Welfare Implications of Gestation Sow Housing" (2015), available online at https://www.avma.org/resources-tools/literature-reviews/welfare-implications-gestation-sow-housing.

46 American Veterinary Medical Association, "Welfare Implications of Swine Castration," *Literature Reviews* (2013), available online at https://www.avma.org/resources-tools/literature-reviews/welfare-implications-swine-castration.

47 D. Temple, E. Mainau, and X. Manteca, "Tail Biting in Pigs," *The Farm Animal Welfare Fact Sheet* 8 (2014), available online at https://www.fawec.org/media/com_lazypdf/pdf/fs8-en.pdf. Note that although these explanations for tail biting are common in the literature, many researchers express uncertainty about the precise causes of this behavior (e.g., Tina Widowski and Stephanie Torrey, "Neonatal Management Practices," *Swine Welfare Fact Sheet* 1, no. 6 (Des Moines, IA: National Pork Board, 2002); John J. McGlone and Mhairi Sutherland, "Is Tail Docking Necessary and, If So, How Long Should the Tail Be?" *Pork Checkoff Research Report: Animal Welfare* NPB #06-183 (Des Moines, IA: National Pork Board, 2009).)

48 Temple et al., "Tail Biting in Pigs."

49 Stephanie Buijs and Ramon Muns, "A Review of the Effects of Non-Straw Enrichment on Tail Biting in Pigs," *Animals* 9, no. 10 (2019): 824.

50 American Veterinary Medical Association, "Welfare Implications of Teeth Clipping, Tail Docking and Permanent Identification of Piglets," *Literature Reviews* (2014), available online at https://www.avma.org/resources-tools/literature-reviews/welfare-implications-teeth-clipping-tail-docking-and-permanent-identification-piglets. Interestingly—and somewhat tragically—one potential explanation for *why* tail docking reduces biting behavior is that it makes pigs more sensitive to being bitten and thus more likely to react when others bite them (McGlone and Sutherland, "Is Tail Docking Necessary?," 8–9).

51 D. Fraser, "Observations on the Behavioural Development of Suckling and Early-Weaned Piglets during the First Six Weeks after Birth," *Animal Behaviour* 26, no. 1 (1978): 22–30; Joy M. Campbell, Joe D. Crenshaw, and Javier Polo, "The Biological Stress of Early Weaned Piglets," *Journal of Animal Science and Biotechnology* 4 (2013), art. 19.

52 H.B. Graves, "Behavior and Ecology of Wild and Feral Swine (Sus scrofa)," *Journal of Animal Science* 58, no. 2 (1984): 482–492.

53 Fraser, "Behavioural Development of Suckling and Early-Weaned Piglets"; Campbell et al., "Biological Stress of Early-Weaned Piglets."

54 N.E. O'Connell, N.E. and V.E. Beattie, "Influence of Environmental Enrichment on Aggressive Behaviour and Dominance Relationships in Growing Pigs," *Animal Welfare* 8, no. 3 (1999): 269–279; V.E. Beattie, N.E. O'Connell, and B.W. Moss, "Influence of Environmental Enrichment on the Behaviour, Performance, and Meat Quality of Domestic Pigs," *Livestock Production Science* 65, nos. 1–2 (2000): 71–79.

55 G.P. Pearce and A.M. Paterson, "The Effect of Space Restriction and Provision of Toys during Rearing on the Behaviour, Productivity, and Physiology of Male Pigs," *Applied Animal Behaviour Science* 36, no. 1 (1993): 11–28.

56 P.H. Hemsworth, J.L. Barnett, C. Hansen, and C.G. Winfield, "Effects of Social Environment on Welfare Status and Sexual Behaviour of Female Pigs II: Effects of Space Allowance," *Applied Animal Behaviour Science* 16, no. 3 (1986): 259–267.

57 Steve Wing, Rachel Avery Horton, Stephen W. Marshall, Kendall Thu, Mansoureh Tajik, Leah Schinasi, and Susan S. Schiffman, "Air Pollution and Odor in Communities Near Industrial Swine Operations," *Environmental Health Perspectives* 116, no. 10 (2008): 1362–1368.

58 Maria C. Mirabelli, Steve Wing, Stephen W. Marshall, and Timothy C. Wilcosky, "Asthma Symptoms among Adolescents Who Attend Public Schools that are Located Near Confined Swine Feeding Operations," *Pediatrics* 118, no. 1 (2006): e66–e75.

59 Michael A. Mallin and Lawrence B. Cahoon, "Industrialized Animal Production—A Major Source of Nutrient and Microbial Pollution to Aquatic Ecosystems," *Population and Environment* 24, no. 5 (2003): 369–385; JoAnn Burkholder, Bob Libra, Peter Weyer, Susan Heathcote, Dana Kolpin, Peter S. Thorne, and Michael Wichman, "Impacts of Waste

from Concentrated Animal Feeding Operations on Water Quality," *Environmental Health Perspectives* 115, no. 2 (2007): 308–312.

60   Centers for Disease Control and Prevention, "2009 H1N1 Pandemic (H1N1pdm09 virus)" (2019), available online at https://www.cdc.gov/flu/pandemic-resources/2009-h1n1-pandemic.html.

61   Benjamin M. Rosenthal, Guiseppe LaRosa, Dante Zarlenga, Detiger Dunams, Yao Chunyu, Liu Mingyuan, and Edoardo Pozio, "Human Dispersal of *Trichinella spiralis* in Domesticated Pigs," *Infection, Genetics and Evolution* 8, no. 6 (2008): 799–805.

62   Hannah C. Lewis, Kåre Mølbak, Catrin Reese, Frank M. Aarestrup, Mette Selchau, Marit Sørum, and Robert L. Skov, "Pigs as Source of Methicillin-Resistant *Staphylococcus aureus* CC398 Infections in Humans, Denmark," *Emerging Infectious Diseases* 14, no. 9 (2008): 1383–1389.

63   William D. McBride and Kenneth Mathews Jr., *The Diverse Structure and Organization of U.S. Beef Cow-Calf Farms* (Washington, D.C.: USDA Economic Research Service 2011), 5.

64   Ibid., 6.

65   Burt Rutherford, "The Calf-Fed Conundrum," *Beef Magazine* (Jan. 30, 2019), available online at https://www.beefmagazine.com/commentary/calf-fed-conundrum.

66   U.S. Department of Agriculture Economic Research Service, "Cattle & Beef: Sector at a Glance" (2020), available online at https://www.ers.usda.gov/topics/animal-products/cattle-beef/sector-at-a-glance/.

67   Bryan McMurray, "Cow Size is Growing," *Beef Magazine* (Feb. 1, 2009), available online at https://www.beefmagazine.com/genetics/0201-increased-beef-cows.

68   For a video presentation of the slaughtering process as viewed through the eyes of the industry, see North American Meat Institute, "Video Tour of a Beef Plant featuring Temple Grandin" (2012), available online at https://www.youtube.com/watch?v=VMqYYXswono.

69   American Veterinary Medical Association, "Welfare Implications of Hot-Iron Branding and Its Alternatives," *AVMA Literature Reviews* (2011), available online at https://www.avma.org/resources-tools/literature-reviews/welfare-implications-hot-iron-branding-and-its-alternatives.

70   Neil Anderson, "Dehorning of Calves," *Ontario Ministry of Agriculture, Food, and Rural Affairs Factsheet* 09-003 (2012), available online at http://www.omafra.gov.on.ca/english/livestock/dairy/facts/09-003.htm; American Veterinary Medical Association, "Welfare Implications of Disbudding and Dehorning Cattle," *AVMA Literature Reviews* (2014), available online at https://www.avma.org/resources-tools/literature-reviews/welfare-implications-dehorning-and-disbudding-cattle.

71   American Veterinary Medical Association, "Welfare Implications of Disbudding and Dehorning Cattle," *AVMA Literature Reviews* (2014), available online at https://www.avma.org/resources-tools/literature-reviews/welfare-implications-dehorning-and-disbudding-cattle;

American Veterinary Medical Association, "Welfare Implications of Castration of Cattle," *AVMA Literature Reviews* (2014), available online https://www.avma.org/resources-tools/literature-reviews/welfare-implications-castration-cattle.

72 T.G. Nagaraja and Kelly F. Lechtenberg, "Acidosis in Feedlot Cattle," *Veterinary Clinics of North America: Food Animal Practice* 23, no. 2 (2007): 333–350.

73 J. Gerber, H. Steinfeld, B. Henderson, A. Mottet, C. Opio, J. Dikman, A. Falcucci, and G. Tempio, *Tackling Climate Change through Livestock: A Global Assessment of Emissions and Mitigation Opportunities* (Rome: Food and Agriculture Organization of the United Nations, 2013), xii.

74 Ibid.

75 Global Institute of Sustainable Forestry, "Cattle Ranching in the Amazon Region," *Global Forest Atlas* (2020), available online at https://globalforestatlas.yale.edu/amazon/land-use/cattle-ranching.

76 In this connection, Mark Budolfson notes in "Consumer Ethics, Harm Footprints, and the Empirical Dimensions of Food Choices," in *Philosophy Comes to Dinner: Arguments about the Ethics of Eating* (New York: Routledge, 2016), 163–181, that if one's concern is specifically to minimize the "pain footprint" of one's eating choices, vegetarianism is likely a sub-optimal strategy relative to eating certain meat products and avoiding certain vegetarian ones. See also Steven L. Davis, "The Least Harm Principle May Require that Humans Consume a Diet Containing Large Herbivores, Not a Vegan Diet," *Journal of Agricultural and Environmental Ethics* 16, no. 4 (2003): 387–394; Bob Fischer, *The Ethics of Eating Meat: Usually Bad, Sometimes Wrong, Often Permissible* (New York: Routledge, 2020), ch. 5.

77 https://www.nimanranch.com.

78 Jonathan Safran Foer, *Eating Animals* (New York: Little, Brown & Co., 2009), 224.

79 Ibid.

80 Ibid., 241–244.

81 It is worth noting in this connection that some people have argued it's objectionable to bring humans into existence because of the badness of their lives. See, e.g., David Benetar, *Better Never to Have Been: The Harm of Coming Into Existence* (New York: Oxford University Press, 2006). With apologies to those who find such views plausible, I will not engage with them here.

82 See, e.g., M.C. Appleby and P.T. Sandøe, "Philosophical Debate on the Nature of Well-being: Implications for Animal Welfare," *Animal Welfare* 11, no. 3 (2002): 283–294; David Fraser, "Understanding Animal Welfare," *Acta Veterinaria Scandinavica* 50 (2008): S1.

83 See, e.g., P.H. Hemsworth, "Key Determinants of Pig Welfare: Implications of Animal Management and Housing Design on Livestock Welfare," *Animal Production Science* 58, no. 8 (2018): 1375–1386.

84 More graphically, several authors have noted that the widespread practice of male circumcision represents a form of physical mutilation

that, when performed improperly, can lead to serious lifelong complications. See, e.g., R.M. Williams, "On the Tail-Docking of Pigs, Human Circumcision, and Their Implications for Prevailing Opinion Regarding Pain," *Journal of Applied Philosophy* 20, no. 1 (2003): 89–93; Thompson, "Philosophical Ethics and the Improvement of Farmed Animal Lives," 25.

85 See on this point Thompson, "Philosophical Ethics and the Improvement of Farmed Animal Lives," 24–26.

86 National Chicken Council, *National Chicken Council Animal Welfare Guidelines and Audit Checklist for Broilers* (Washington, DC: National Chicken Council, 2019); National Pork Board, *Common Swine Industry Audit: Instructions, Standards, and Audit Tool* (Des Moines, IA: National Pork Board, 2021); National Cattlemen's Beef Association, *Beef Quality Assurance: National Manual* (Centennial, CO: National Cattlemen's Beef Association, 2019); North American Meat Institute, *Recommended Animal Handling Guidelines & Audit Guide: A Systematic Approach to Animal Welfare* (Washington, DC: North American Meat Institute, 2019).

87 Professional Animal Auditor Certification Organization, "Leadership: Founding Members, Board of Directors, Committees & Staff" (2021), available online at https://animalauditor.org/About/Members.

88 See National Chicken Council, *Welfare Guidelines and Audit Checklist*.

89 Ibid., 1.

90 Ibid., 3.

91 Ibid.

92 Ibid., 5.

93 Ibid., 6.

94 Ibid., 11.

95 Ibid.

96 Ibid., 10.

97 National Pork Board, *Common Swine Industry Audit*, 13–14.

98 Ibid., 12.

99 Ibid., 13.

100 Graves, "Wild and Feral Swine," 483; A. Stolba and D.G.M. Wood-Gush, "The Identification of Behavioural Key Features and their Incorporation into a Housing Design for Pigs," *Annales de Recherches Vétérinaires* 15, no. 2 (1984): 287–302, at 292.

101 American Humane, *American Humane Certified Animal Welfare Standards for Swine* (Washington, DC: American Humane, 2017), 19; Humane Farm Animal Care, *Humane Farm Animal Care Animal Care Standards, January 2018: Pigs* (Middleburg, VA: Humane Farm Animal Care, 2018), 19; A Greener World, *Certified Animal Welfare Approved by AGW Standards for Pigs* (Terrebonne, OR: A Greener World, 2020), 11; Global Animal Partnership, *Global Animal Partnership's 5-Step Animal Welfare Standards for Pigs v2.4* (Austin, TX: Global Animal Partnership, 2020), 18. A Greener World, in "Nose Ringing Pigs," *A Greener World Technical Advice Fact Sheet*

16 (2020), available online at https://agreenerworld.org/wp-content/uploads/2020/05/TAFS-16-Nose-Ringing-Pigs-v4.pdf, notes one possible exception: "the standards will permit one septum nose ring for breeding sows if it can be demonstrated that the activity of the sow [i.e., in digging a nest for her offspring] would otherwise damage the soil structure, cause environmental pollution, or compromise the welfare of the litter. No other pigs may be nose ringed and farms entering the program that wish to nose ring must be able to demonstrate the environmental or other risk factors, and why this cannot be managed in any other way."

102 National Chicken Council, *Welfare Guidelines and Audit Checklist*, 13.

103 American Humane, *American Humane Certified Animal Welfare Standards* for Broiler Chickens (Washington, DC: American Humane, 2019), 21; Humane Farm Animal Care, *Humane Farm Animal Care Animal Care Standards, August 2014: Chickens* (Middleburg, VA: Humane Farm Animal Care, 2018), 24; Global Animal Partnership, *Global Animal Partnership's 5-Step Animal Welfare Rating Standards* for Chickens Raised for Meat v3.1 (Austin, TX: Global Animal Partnership, 2017), 28. For American Humane and Humane Farm Animal Care, the limit is three birds per hand, regardless of weight. Global Animal Partnership sets the limit at four birds per hand for its Steps 1–4. Step 5 limits catchers to two birds per hand, and Step 5+ requires each chicken to be caught and carried individually in an upright position.

104 Consumer Reports National Research Center, *Food Labels Survey: 2016 Nationally-Representative Phone Survey* (Washington, DC: Consumer Reports, 2016), 16.

105 American Humane, *Standards for Broiler Chickens*, 8; American Humane, *Standards for Swine*; Humane Farm Animal Care, *Chickens*, 10; Humane Farm Animal Care, *Pigs*.

106 A Greener World, *Animal Welfare Approved Standards* for Meat Chickens (Terrebonne, OR: A Greener World, 2018), 12–15; A Greener World, *Standards for Pigs*, 12–15.

107 Global Animal Partnership, *Standards for Chickens*, 25–27; Global Animal Partnership, *Standards for Pigs*, 31–32.

108 National Chicken Council, *Welfare Guidelines and Audit Checklist*, 12.

109 American Humane, *Standards for Broiler Chickens*, 6.

110 Humane Farm Animal Care, *Chickens*, 6.

111 A Greener World, *Standards for Meat Chickens*, 17.

112 Global Animal Partnership, *Standards for Chickens*, 8.

113 National Chicken Council, *Welfare Guidelines and Audit Checklist*, 11.

114 American Humane, *Standards for Broiler Chickens*, 20.

115 Global Animal Partnership, *Standards for Chickens*, 28; Humane Farm Animal Care, *Chickens*, 29.

116 A Greener World, *Standards for Meat Chickens*, 27.

117 AGreenerWorld,"CertifiedAnimalWelfareStandardsApprovedbyAGW" (2020), available online at https://agreenerworld.org/certifications/animal-welfare-approved/standards/.

118 A Greener World, "Find Certified Products" (2021), available at https://agreenerworld.org/directory/.

119 AmericanHumane,"CertifiedProducers:Meat"(2021),availableonline at http://www.humaneheartland.org/humane-certified-producers/category/meat.

120 Humane Farm Animal Care, "Producers who are Certified Humane" (2021), available online at https://certifiedhumane.org/whos-certified-2/.

121 Global Animal Partnership, "For Shoppers" (2021), available online at https://globalanimalpartnership.org/shoppers/.

122 American Humane, *Standards for Broiler Chickens*, ii.

123 American Humane, *Standards for Swine*, v; American Humane, *Standards for Beef Cattle*, v.

124 WATTPoultryUSA, "2021 Top Poultry Companies" (March 2021), 21, available online at https://www.wattpoultryusa-digital.com/wattpoultryusa/march_2021/.

125 Perdue Foods, "Programs and Practices" (2021), available online at https://corporate.perduefarms.com/responsibility/animal-care/programs-practices/.

126 Global Animal Partnership, "For Producers" (2021), available online at https://globalanimalpartnership.org/producers/.

127 U.S. Department of Agriculture National Agricultural Statistics Service, "Agriculture Counts: Cattle" (Jan. 2021), available online at https://www.nass.usda.gov/Publications/Todays_Reports/reports/catl0121.pdf; U.S. Department of Agriculture National Agricultural Statistics Service, "Quarterly Hogs and Pigs" (Mar. 2021), available online at https://downloads.usda.library.cornell.edu/usda-esmis/files/rj430453j/7p88db205/mw22w1890/hgpg0321.pdf; National Chicken Council, "Broiler Chicken Industry Key Facts 2020."

MAKING A DIFFERENCE

1 It's worth noting in this connection that some vegetarians do see these efficacy-based arguments as central to their views. For example, Peter Singer writes, in *Animal Liberation, Updated Edition* (New York: HarperCollins, [1975] 1999), 161: "Becoming a vegetarian is not merely a symbolic gesture. Nor is it an attempt to isolate oneself from the ugly realities of the world, to keep oneself pure and so without responsibility for the cruelty and carnage all around. Becoming a vegetarian is a highly practical and effective step one can take toward ending both the killing of nonhuman animals and the infliction of suffering upon them."

2 This is to say I didn't directly "hire" anyone to produce these products for me. A number of vegetarian authors have plausibly noted that insofar as we agree mainstream meat industry practices are wrong, we should infer it's also wrong to "hire" people to engage in those practices on one's behalf. See, e.g., Mylan Engel, "The Commonsense Case for Ethical Vegetarianism," *Between the Species* 19, no. 1 (2016): 2–31, at 4–5; Michael Huemer, *Dialogues on Ethical Vegetarianism* (New York: Routledge, 2019), 25–27. These arguments fail not because they're mistaken about the ethics of hiring people to engage in wrongdoing but rather because ordinary acts of consumption in the marketplace don't constitute instances of "hiring" people to do things. When I hire someone to perform an immoral act, the person performs the act in question *at my behest*. But nothing like this happens when I purchase a pre-existing cut of meat at the supermarket or order a dish containing pre-existing pieces of meat at a restaurant.

3 The discussion below follows and elaborates upon Mark Bryant Budolfson's exposition in "Is It Wrong to Eat Meat from Factory Farms? If So, Why?" in Ben Bramble and Bob Fischer (eds), *The Moral Complexities of Eating Meat* (New York: Oxford University Press, 2016), 80–98.

4 For further discussion of this idea, see Bob Fischer, *The Ethics of Eating Animals: Usually Bad, Sometimes Wrong, Often Permissible* (New York: Routledge, 2020), 60.

5 Jean C. Buzby, Hodan Farah Wells, Bruce Axtman, and Jana Mickey, "Supermarket Loss Estimates for Fresh Fruit, Vegetables, Meat, Poultry, and Seafood and Their Use in the ERS Loss-Adjusted Food Availability Data," *USDA Economic Information Bulletin* 44 (2009), 14. Even higher loss numbers are reported using different analytical methods by Jean C. Buzby, Jeanine T. Bentley, Beth Padera, Jennifer Campuzano, and Cara Ammon, "Updated Supermarket Shrink Estimates for Fresh Foods and Their Implications for ERS Loss-Adjusted Food Availability Data," *USDA Economic Information Bulletin* 155 (2016).

6 See on this point Julia Nefsky, "Consequentialism and the Problem of Collective Harm: A Reply to Kagan," *Philosophy & Public Affairs* 39, no. 4 (2011): 364–395, at 370.

7 In the literature on the ethics of eating meat, much ink has been spilled on examining an alternative pathway by which individuals' dietary choices may be swallowed up before being transmitted higher up the supply chain. This pathway has to do with the fact that some meat products are sold in bulk, such that supermarkets order them in *boxes* or *cases* rather than individual units. If steaks come in boxes of 100, then most of the time, a single consumer's decision to buy steak will not trigger any additional meat to be ordered. Yet, as several vegetarian authors have noted, this fact on its own cannot vindicate the Inefficacy Thesis, since for all this tells us, each consumer could still have a roughly proportionate chance of causing an entire box of steaks to be ordered.

If buying a steak causes nothing to happen 99% of the time and a box of 100 steaks to be ordered 1% of the time, then the *average* result of buying a steak will be that an additional steak is ordered. See on this point Peter Singer, "Utilitarianism and Vegetarianism," *Philosophy & Public Affairs* 9, no. 4 (1980): 325–337, at 334–336; Alistair Norcross, "Puppies, Pigs, and People: Eating Meat and Marginal Cases," *Philosophical Perspectives* 18 (2004): 229–245, at 232–233; David DeGrazia, "Moral Vegetarianism from a Very Broad Basis," *Journal of Moral Philosophy* 6, no. 2 (2009): 143–165, at 158; Shelly Kagan, "Do I Make a Difference?" *Philosophy & Public Affairs* 39, no. 2 (2011): 105–141, at 121–127; Michael Huemer, *Dialogues on Ethical Vegetarianism* (New York: Routledge, 2019), 27–29. The point I have been making in this section is independent of whether meat products are ordered individually or in bulk. My focus is on the fact that meat ordering decisions are typically made on a regular schedule according to expected future needs, not in reaction to individual consumer purchases. It is worth noting, however, that insofar as many retailers would sooner go without a marginal sale than purchase an entire box of meat they weren't expecting to need, the fact that meat products are often sold in bulk may sometimes present an additional reason why an individual's purchasing decision can fail to be transmitted any further up the supply chain. For further discussion, see Nefsky, "Consequentialism and the Problem of Collective Harm"; Mark Bryant Budolfson, "The Inefficacy Objection to Consequentialism and the Problem with the Expected Consequences Response," *Philosophical Studies* 176, no. 7 (2019): 1711–1724.

8 Budolfson, "The Inefficacy Objection to Consequentialism," 1718.
9 For budget examples for several different kinds of livestock operations, see Glynn Tonsor and Robin Reid, "Livestock Budgets," *AgManager.info* (2020), available online at https://www.agmanager.info/farm-mgmt-guides/livestock-budgets.
10 Gary Chartier, "On the Threshold Argument against Consumer Meat Purchases," *Journal of Social Philosophy* 37, no. 2 (2006): 233–249, at 242–243.
11 Ben Almassi, in "The Consequences of Individual Consumption: A Defense of Threshold Arguments for Vegetarianism and Consumer Ethics," *Journal of Applied Philosophy* 28, no. 4 (2011): 396–411, argues that as long as there is *some* (i.e., non-zero) chance an act of consumption will make a difference to production decisions, there remains "a consequentialist basis" for abstaining from meat, "all other things being equal" (403). Almassi is correct that, in cases where a person is utterly indifferent between eating meat and abstaining (i.e., all other things are truly equal), the infinitesimal probability of reducing total meat production would break the tie in favor of vegetarianism. But of course, meat-eaters typically eat meat because they prefer to do so, and thus all other things are generally not equal in the way his argument requires.

Moreover, in *The Ethics of Eating Animals*, Bob Fischer perceptively argues that in cases where consumers *do* affect meat industry operations, there's no guarantee these impacts will be morally desirable. For example, producers could respond to unexpectedly bad market conditions by cutting corners and eking out better margins wherever possible—even if this meant sacrificing measures they ordinarily take to protect their animals, their workers, the environment, or public health (64–68; see likewise Philip E. Devine, "The Moral Basis of Vegetarianism," *Philosophy* 53, no. 206 (1978): 481–505, at 484). I don't foreground these perverse potentialities since, for reasons we've discussed, they virtually never occur. But they bear mentioning to forestall the misimpression that only neutral or positive outcomes can result from abstaining from meat. Just as it's *possible*—though exceedingly unlikely—for a consumer to exacerbate the meat industry's problems by eating meat, so too is it possible—and exceedingly unlikely—for a consumer to exacerbate these problems by becoming a vegetarian.

12 Singer, *Animal Liberation*, 163–164.
13 The Humane Research Council, "Study of Current and Former Vegetarians and Vegans" (2014), available online at https://faunalytics.org/wp-content/uploads/2015/06/Faunalytics_Current-Former-Vegetarians_Full-Report.pdf.
14 Bailey F. Norwood and Jason F. Lusk, in *Compassion, by the Pound: The Economics of Farm Animal Welfare* (New York: Oxford University Press, 2011), 221–224, report that on average, each pound of meat consumers abstain from eating results in between 0.68–0.91 fewer pounds being produced over the long run. The relationship is not one to one because, rather than reducing production, meat companies can also respond to reduced demand by lowering their prices, thereby attracting customers who would not have bought at higher rates. Even if vegetarians don't prevent the production of quite as much meat as they personally abstain from consuming, their impact on overall production is still considerable. However, as Bob Fischer emphasizes in *The Ethics of Eating Animals*, 61, figures like these are calculated by comparing overall levels of meat consumption and production at given price levels and do not represent the expected marginal impact of a single person deciding to become a vegetarian.
15 See on this point Julia Nefsky, "How You Can Help, Without Making A Difference," *Philosophical Studies* 174, no. 11 (2017): 2743–2767.
16 See along these lines Singer, *Animal Liberation*, 220–221; Almassi, "The Consequences of Individual Consumption," 398; Huemer, *Dialogues on Ethical Vegetarianism*, 50–51.
17 E.g., Huemer, *Dialogues on Ethical Vegetarianism*, 51–53.
18 U.S. Department of Agriculture National Agricultural Statistics Service, "Agriculture Counts: Cattle" (Jan. 2021), available online at https://www.nass.usda.gov/Publications/Todays_Reports/reports/

catl0121.pdf; U.S. Department of Agriculture National Agricultural Statistics Service, "Quarterly Hogs and Pigs" (Mar. 2021), available online at https://downloads.usda.library.cornell.edu/usda-esmis/files/rj430453j/7p88db205/mw22w1890/hgpg0321.pdf; National Chicken Council, "Broiler Chicken Industry Key Facts 2020."

19 Even beyond the actual burdens imposed by social frictions, many people report apprehension toward being stigmatized as a reason not to give up eating meat. See, e.g., Kelly L. Markowski and Susan Roxburgh, "'If I Became a Vegan, My Family and Friends Would Hate Me:' Anticipating Vegan Stigma as a Barrier to Plant-Based Diets," *Appetite* 135 (2019): 1–9. Cheryl Abbate, "Meat Eating and Moral Responsibility: Exploring the Moral Distinctions between Meat Eaters and Puppy Torturers," *Utilitas* 32, no. 4 (2020): 398–415, describes these social frictions as a kind of "cultural duress."

20 Humane Research Council, "Study of Current and Former Vegetarians and Vegans," 7.

21 Hannah Ritchie and Max Roser, "Meat and Dairy Production," *Our World in Data* (2019), available online at https://ourworldindata.org/meat-production.

22 See on this point Singer, *Animal Liberation*, 161–164.

23 See on this point Devine, "The Moral Basis of Vegetarianism," 483–484.

24 In this connection, it's striking to note how little effort vegetarians devote to political advocacy. According to OpenSecrets.org, the US meat industry contributed $42 million in 2020 to the campaigns of federal candidates and spent another $9.5 million on lobbying. See "Livestock" (2021), available online at https://www.opensecrets.org/industries/indus.php?ind=A06++; "Poultry & Eggs" (2020), available online at https://www.opensecrets.org/industries/indus.php?ind=A05++; and "Meat Processing & Products" (2020), available online at https://www.opensecrets.org/industries/indus.php?ind=G2300.

25 See, e.g., Megan Earle and Gordon Hodson, "What's Your Beef with Vegetarians? Predicting Anti-Vegetarian Prejudice from Pro-Beef Attitudes across Cultures," *Personality and Individual Differences* 119 (2017): 52–55; Cara C. MacInnis and Gordon Hodson, "It Ain't Easy Eating Greens: Evidence of Bias toward Vegetarians and Vegans from Both Source and Target," *Group Processes & Intergroup Relations* 20, no. 6 (2017): 721–744. If one million vegetarians were willing to donate just $10 per week to support their cause in politics, this would generate $520 million per year—more than ten times as much as the American meat industry spent in a presidential election year. In reality, however, relatively few vegetarians translate their activism into aggressive political advocacy, with the result that industry players routinely dwarf their political influence.

26 Neilsen Retail Measurement Services, "Meet the New 'Meat' Eater" (Aug. 5, 2019), available online at https://www.nielsen.com/us/en/insights/article/2019/meet-the-new-meat-eater/.

27 See on this point Singer, *Animal Liberation*, 220–221.

WHAT IF EVERYONE DID THAT?

1 The most famous articulation of this idea comes from Immanuel Kant, *Groundwork of the Metaphysics of Morals*, translated and edited by Mary Gregor (New York: Cambridge University Press, [1785] 2006). Similar views, however, have been presented by writers broadly working in the consequentialist tradition, e.g., Brad Hooker, *Ideal Code, Real World: A Rule-Consequentialist Theory of Morality* (New York: Oxford University Press, 2000).

2 For discussion of this line of reasoning, see, e.g., Dan Egonsson, "Kant's Vegetarianism," *Journal of Value Inquiry* 31 (1997): 473–483, at 473–477; Michael J. Almeida and Mark H. Bernstein, "Opportunistic Carnivorism," *Journal of Applied Philosophy* 17, no. 2 (2000): 205–211, at 207.

3 I'll note that, as a logical matter, we need to interpret the universalization test in a particular way for this objection to get off the ground. If *literally everyone* behaved as most meat-eaters do—by purchasing and eating meat when it's available but not producing it themselves—nothing objectionable would result since no one would be *producing* meat in this scenario. For the objection to work, we need to imagine a world in which people *generally* behave they way meat-eaters do, but some people produce the products that satisfy these people's desires. For further discussion of the need to interpret the universalization test in terms of less-than-perfect compliance, see Hooker, *Ideal Code, Real World*.

4 As Tristram McPherson contends in "Why I Am a Vegan (And Why You Should Be One Too)," in *Philosophy Comes to Dinner: Arguments about the Ethics of Eating*, edited by Andrew Chignell, Terence Cuneo, and Matthew C. Halteman (New York: Routledge, 2016), 73–91, at 81, this obligation is plausibly rendered as a duty of "fair play" to make a fair contribution to successful cooperative institutions from which one benefits. See along similar lines David DeGrazia, "Vegetarianism from a Very Broad Moral Basis," *Journal of Moral Philosophy* 6, no. 2 (2009), 143–165, at 158–159; Jacob Barrett and Sarah Raskoff, "Ethical Veganism and Free-Riding," unpublished manuscript.

5 The discussion below expands upon Mark Bryant Budolfson's analysis in "The Inefficacy Objection to Consequentialism and the Problem with the Expected Consequences Response," *Philosophical Studies* 176, no. 7 (2019): 1711–1724.

6 For a brief introduction to game theory more broadly, see Gerald F. Gaus, *On Philosophy, Politics, and Economics* (Belmont, CA: Thomson Wadsworth, 2008), ch. 4.

7 This name comes from a fleeting comment in Jean-Jacques Rousseau, *Discourse on the Origin of Inequality*, translated by Donald A. Cress

(Indianapolis, IN: Hackett Publishing, 1992), 47. Note that my explication of this game is designed not to align with Rousseau's original example but rather to make intuitive the structure of payoffs that defines the modern game-theoretic "Stag Hunt."

8 See on this point Julia Nefsky, "How You Can Help, Without Making A Difference," *Philosophical Studies* 174, no. 11 (2017): 2743–2767, at 2748.

9 K.C. Taylor, "Automobile Catalytic Converters," *Studies in Surface Science and Catalysis* 30 (1987): 97–116.

10 See on this point Russ Shafer-Landau, "Vegetarianism, Causation and Ethical Theory," *Public Affairs Quarterly* 8, no. 1 (1994): 85–100, at 93–95.

11 For further discussion of the dynamics of conditional cooperation, see Christina Bicchieri, *The Grammar of Society* (New York: Cambridge University Press, 2006).

12 This outlook helps us see why this book's arguments don't undermine other important collective practices in which individuals make no significant difference, such as voting. In functioning democratic societies, a case for voting can be mustered by observing that this is in fact what enables democracy to work. The key point is that the strength of these arguments is importantly tied to the fact enough people do vote, such that meaningful democratic decisions actually do get made. If we imagine ourselves in a society where virtually nobody voted and hence the outcomes of elections were widely regarded as illegitimate, it seems much less obvious there would be a moral duty for us to vote. (On the other hand, it's worth noting in passing that some people question the value of voting, e.g., Jason Brennan, *The Ethics of Voting* (Princeton, NJ: Princeton University Press, 2011); Christopher Freiman, *Why It's OK to Ignore Politics* (New York: Routledge, 2021).)

13 It is likewise true that, in a world with little cooperation, each person who does not cooperate helps reinforce the noncooperative behavior of others. See on this point Julia Driver, "Individual Consumption and Moral Complicity," in *The Moral Complexities of Eating Meat*, edited by Bob Fischer and Ben Bramble (Oxford University Press, 2016), 67–79, at 75.

14 Ben Almassi, "The Consequences of Individual Consumption: A Defense of Threshold Arguments for Vegetarianism and Consumer Ethics," *Journal of Applied Philosophy* 28, no. 4 (2011): 396–411, at 404–407.

HANGING OUR HATS

1 Jonathan Safran Foer, *Eating Animals* (New York: Little, Brown & Co., 2009), 261.

2 Julia Driver, "Individual Consumption and Moral Complicity," in *The Moral Complexities of Eating Meat*, edited by Ben Bramble and Bob Fischer (New York: Oxford University Press, 2016), 67–79, at 67.

3 Cheshire Calhoun, "Standing for Something," *The Journal of Philosophy* 92, no. 5 (1995): 235–260.

4 For discussion of how even non-obnoxious fixation on one's ethical worldview can undermine cooperation in the face of diversity, see David Schmidtz, "Natural Enemies: An Anatomy of Environmental Conflict," *Environmental Ethics* 22, no. 4 (2000): 397–408.

5 For discussion of how these points bear on the case for vegetarianism, see Mark Bryant Budolfson, "Is It Wrong to Eat Meat from Factory Farms? If So, Why?" in *The Moral Complexities of Eating Meat*, edited by Ben Bramble and Bob Fischer (New York: Oxford University Press, 2016), 80–98, at 89–90. In a complementary line of argument, Marta Zaraska, in "Meeting Meat-Eaters Halfway: Why Reducetarianism Works Better Than Moralizing," *Breakthrough Journal* 10 (2019), available online at https://thebreakthrough.org/journal/no-10-winter-2019/meeting-meat-eaters-halfway, suggests that in light of the common propensity for people to shut down in the face of vegetarian arguments, it may be possible to get people to eat less meat overall by encouraging them to reduce rather than eliminate their consumption. For more on the case for reducing but not eliminating meat production, see Simon Fairlie, *Meat: A Benign Extravagance* (White River Junction, VT: Chelsea Green, 2010).

6 In *The Ethics of Eating Animals*, Bob Fischer notes that people who have chosen to focus their activism in certain ways can thereby acquire strong reasons to behave in ways that support those choices—including by taking actions recommended mainly by others' expectations. Fischer illustrates this by highlighting the many expectations that fall upon his wife, who is politically active in her community. He writes that his wife "is now expected to be present and vocal in ways that she wasn't previously … She certainly thinks that she ought to put up signs and do some leafleting. [However, s]he doesn't think that she has an obligation to put a bumper sticker on her car" (159). Fischer notes expectations like these are largely contingent and not explained by any independent underlying principle of how activists ought to behave. But in his view, the fact his wife has taken a certain role in her community provides powerful reasons—even *obligations*—to behave in conformance with expectations like these. By the same token, Fischer thinks certain kinds of activists can have an obligation to become vegetarians, since this is what is expected of them, though with the caveat that there's no corresponding obligation to become such an activist in the first place (160–161; see in a similar spirit Peter Singer, "Utilitarianism and Vegetarianism," *Philosophy & Public Affairs* 9, no. 4 (1980): 325–337, at 336–337). I might add to Fischer's position the further caveat that people may sometimes have good reasons to *resist* expectations like these (for example, to prove to others that caring about the meat industry's problems is not just a "vegetarian thing"). But I take his point that, for people who have organized their lives around certain forms of

activism, continuing to eat meat would manifest a certain kind of practical irrationality that would push in favor of either becoming vegetarian or shifting course to a different form of activism.

7 See along these lines Russ Shafer-Landau, "Vegetarianism, Causation and Ethical Theory," *Public Affairs Quarterly* 8, no. 1 (1994): 85–100; Terence Cuneo, "Conscientious Omnivorism," in *Philosophy Comes to Dinner: Arguments about the Ethics of Eating*, edited by Andrew Chignell, Terence Cuneo, and Matthew C. Halteman (New York: Routledge, 2016), 21–38, at 25. Julia Driver goes a step further in "Individual Consumption and Moral Complicity," 75, noting that we don't need to interpret meat-eating as a literal expression of endorsement for it to *seem* like endorsement: a person who eats meat "seems to endorse the practice of killing and eating animals, even if she does not in fact endorse the practice of killing and eating animals." I take it, however, that Driver's observation is adequately addressed by the previous section. See also Bob Fischer, *The Ethics of Eating Animals: Usually Bad, Sometimes Wrong, Often Permissible* (New York: Routledge, 2020), 96.

8 Julia Nefsky, "How You Can Help, Without Making A Difference," *Philosophical Studies* 174, no. 11 (2017): 2743–2767.

9 E.g., Driver, "Individual Consumption and Moral Complicity"; Tristam McPherson, "Why I Am a Vegan (and You Should Be One Too)," in *Philosophy Comes to Dinner: Arguments about the Ethics of Eating*, edited by Andrew Chignell, Terence Cuneo, and Matthew C. Halteman (New York: Routledge, 2016), 73–91; Michael Huemer, *Dialogues on Ethical Vegetarianism* (New York: Routledge, 2019), 33–34.

10 Ted A. Warfield, "Eating Dead Animals: Meat Eating, Meat Purchasing, and Proving Too Much," in *Philosophy Comes to Dinner: Arguments about the Ethics of Eating*, edited by Andrew Chignell, Terence Cuneo, and Matthew C. Halteman (New York: Routledge, 2016), 151–162, at 156.

11 Budolfson, "Is It Wrong to Eat Meat from Factory Farms?" 93.

12 This idea of striving to reduce complicity—if perhaps not eliminate it—has appealed to a number of writers in the context of the meat issue and beyond. See, e.g., Driver, "Individual Consumption and Moral Complicity," 78–79; Ty Raterman, "Bearing the Weight of the World: On the Extent of an Individual's Environmental Responsibility," *Environmental Values* 21, no. 4 (2012): 417–436.

13 For discussion of the role played by notions of purity in vegetarians' moral psychology, see Neil Levy, "Vegetarianism: Toward Ideological Impurity," in *The Moral Complexities of Eating Meat*, edited by Ben Bramble and Bob Fischer (New York: Oxford University Press, 2016), 172–184.

14 Emily Atkin, "Al Gore's Carbon Footprint Doesn't Matter," *The New Republic* (Aug. 7, 2017), available online at https://newrepublic.com/article/144199/al-gores-carbon-footprint-doesnt-matter.

15 Sy Montgomery, *Temple Grandin: How the Girl Who Loved Cows Embraced Autism and Changed the World* (Boston: Houghton Mifflin Harcourt, 2012).

16 These statements do not imply endorsement of all aspects of Grandin's relationship to the issue of meat-eating. In particular, one dimension of this relationship that has received striking criticism has to do with Grandin's efforts (or lack thereof) to articulate a robust moral defense of eating meat. As Andy Lamey has noted in "The Animal Ethics of Temple Grandin: A Protectionist Analysis," *Journal of Agricultural and Environmental Ethics* 32, no. 1 (2019): 143–164, Grandin has not been a particularly sophisticated participant in debates over the ethics of vegetarianism, mainly rehashing unpersuasive arguments along the lines we examined in Chapter 1. See, e.g., Temple Grandin and Benjamin Hale, "An Interview with Temple Grandin," *Conjunctions* 61 (2013): 109–119, at 111. It's Grandin's approach to activism, and not her general ethical outlook, that I take to be relevant to this chapter's discussion.

17 Driver, "Individual Consumption and Moral Complicity," 74.

18 For discussion of these points in a different context, see Thomas E. Hill Jr., "Ideals of Human Excellence and Preserving Natural Environments," *Environmental Ethics* 5, no. 3 (1983): 211–224.

19 This idea that meat-eating involves a kind of "forgetting" is a central theme in Foer, *Eating Animals*.

20 For an overview of this idea of "fittingness," see Daniel Jacobson, "Fitting Attitude Theories of Value," *Stanford Encyclopedia of Philosophy* (2011), available online at https://plato.stanford.edu/entries/fitting-attitude-theories/.

21 Asking this question raises what value theorists call the "wrong kind of reason problem." See ibid. I will not discuss this issue in this book, but I'll note for theoretically inclined readers that those who are preoccupied by it may resist my reasoning in what follows.

Bibliography

A Greener World, *Animal Welfare Approved Standards for Meat Chickens* (Terrebonne, OR: A Greener World, 2018).

A Greener World, *Certified Animal Welfare Approved by AGW Standards for Pigs* (Terrebonne, OR: A Greener World, 2020a).

A Greener World, "Nose Ringing Pigs," *A Greener World Technical Advice Fact Sheet* 16 (2020b), available online at https://agreenerworld.org/wp-content/uploads/2020/05/TAFS-16-Nose-Ringing-Pigs-v4.pdf.

A Greener World, "Certified Animal Welfare Standards Approved by AGW" (2020c), available online at https://agreenerworld.org/certifications/animal-welfare-approved/standards/.

A Greener World, "Find Certified Products" (2021), available online at https://agreenerworld.org/directory/.

Abbate, Cheryl, "Save the Meat for Cats: Why It's Wrong to Eat Roadkill," *Journal of Agricultural and Environmental Ethics* 32, no. 1 (2019): 165–182.

Abbate, Cheryl, "Meat Eating and Moral Responsibility: Exploring the Moral Distinctions between Meat Eaters and Puppy Torturers," *Utilitas* 32, no. 4 (2020): 398–415.

Al Homidan, A., J.F. Robertson, and A.M. Petchey, "Review of the Effect of Ammonia and Dust Concentrations on Broiler Performance," *World's Poultry Science Journal* 59, no. 3 (2003): 340–349.

Almassi, Ben, "The Consequences of Individual Consumption: A Defense of Threshold Arguments for Vegetarianism and Consumer Ethics," *Journal of Applied Philosophy* 28, no. 4 (2011): 396–411.

Almeida, Michael J. and Mark H. Bernstein, "Opportunistic Carnivorism," *Journal of Applied Philosophy* 17, no. 2 (2000): 205–211.

American Humane, *American Humane Certified Animal Welfare Standards for Swine* (Washington, DC: American Humane, 2017).

American Humane, *American Humane Certified Animal Welfare Standards for Broiler Chickens* (Washington, DC: American Humane, 2019).

American Humane, "Certified Producers: Meat" (2021), available online at http://www.humaneheartland.org/humane-certified-producers/category/meat.

American Veterinary Medical Association, "Welfare Implications of Hot-Iron Branding and Its Alternatives," *AVMA Literature Reviews* (2011), available online at https://www.avma.org/resources-tools/literature-reviews/welfare-implications-hot-iron-branding-and-its-alternatives.

American Veterinary Medical Association, "Welfare Implications of Swine Castration," *Literature Reviews* (2013), available online at https://www.avma.org/resources-tools/literature-reviews/welfare-implications-swine-castration.

American Veterinary Medical Association, "Welfare Implications of Castration of Cattle," *AVMA Literature Reviews* (2014a), available online at https://www.avma.org/resources-tools/literature-reviews/welfare-implications-castration-cattle.

American Veterinary Medical Association, "Welfare Implications of Disbudding and Dehorning Cattle," *AVMA Literature Reviews* (2014b), available online at https://www.avma.org/resources-tools/literature-reviews/welfare-implications-dehorning-and-disbudding-cattle.

American Veterinary Medical Association, "Welfare Implications of Teeth Clipping, Tail Docking and Permanent Identification of Piglets," *Literature Reviews* (2014c), available online at https://www.avma.org/resources-tools/literature-reviews/welfare-implications-teeth-clipping-tail-docking-and-permanent-identification-piglets.

American Veterinary Medical Association, "Welfare Implications of Gestation Sow Housing" (2015), available online at https://www.avma.org/resources-tools/literature-reviews/welfare-implications-gestation-sow-housing.

Anderson, Elizabeth, "Animal Rights and the Values of Nonhuman Life," in *Animal Rights: Current Debates and New Directions*, edited by Cass R. Sunstein and Martha Nussbaum (New York: Oxford University Press, 2004), 277–298.

Anderson, Neil, "Dehorning of Calves," *Ontario Ministry of Agriculture, Food, and Rural Affairs Factsheet* 09-003 (2012), available online at http://www.omafra.gov.on.ca/english/livestock/dairy/facts/09-003.htm.

Anomaly, Jonathan, "What's Wrong with Factory Farming?" *Public Health Ethics* 8, no. 3 (2015): 246–254.

Appleby, M.C. and P.T. Sandøe, "Philosophical Debate on the Nature of Well-being: Implications for Animal Welfare," *Animal Welfare* 11, no. 3 (2002): 283–294.

Atkin, Emily, "Al Gore's Carbon Footprint Doesn't Matter," *The New Republic* (Aug. 7, 2017), available online at https://newrepublic.com/article/144199/al-gores-carbon-footprint-doesnt-matter.

Why It's OK to Eat Meat

Augustine, *On Genesis*, translated by Edmund Hill and edited by John E. Rotelle (New City Press, 2002).

Baker, B.I., S. Torrey, T.M. Widowski, P.V. Turner, T.D. Knezacek, J. Nicholds, T.G. Crowe, and K. Schwean-Lardner, "Evaluation of Carbon Dioxide Induction Methods for the Euthanasia of Day-Old Cull Broiler Chicks," *Poultry Science* 98, no. 5 (2019): 2043–2053.

Barrett, Jacob and Sarah Raskoff, "Ethical Veganism and Free-Riding," unpublished manuscript.

Basinas, Ioannis, Torben Sigsgaard, Hans Kromhout, Dick Heederik, Inge M. Wouters, and Vivi Schlünssen, "A Comprehensive Review of Levels and Determinants of Personal Exposure to Dust and Endotoxin in Livestock Farming," *Journal of Exposure Science and Environmental Epidemiology* 25, no. 2 (2015): 123–137.

Beattie, V.E., N.E. O'Connell, and B.W. Moss, "Influence of Environmental Enrichment on the Behaviour, Performance, and Meat Quality of Domestic Pigs," *Livestock Production Science* 65, nos. 1–2 (2000): 71–79.

Belshaw, Christopher, "Meat," in *The Moral Complexities of Eating Meat*, edited by Ben Bramble and Bob Fischer (New York: Oxford University Press, 2016), 9–29.

Benetar, David, *Better Never to Have Been: The Harm of Coming Into Existence* (New York: Oxford University Press, 2006).

Benson, G. John and Bernard E. Rollin, *The Well-being of Farm Animals: Challenges and Solutions* (Ames, IA: Blackwell, 2004).

Bessei, W., "Welfare of Broilers: A Review," *World's Poultry Science Journal* 62, no. 3 (2006): 455–466.

Bicchieri, Christina, *The Grammar of Society* (New York: Cambridge University Press, 2006).

Biesalski, H.K., "Meat as a Component of a Healthy Diet—Are There Any Risks or Benefits if Meat Is Avoided in the Diet?" *Meat Science* 70, no. 3 (2005): 509–524.

Brennan, Jason, *The Ethics of Voting* (Princeton, NJ: Princeton University Press, 2011).

Bruckner, Donald W., "Strict Vegetarianism Is Immoral," in *The Moral Complexities of Eating Meat*, edited by Ben Bramble and Bob Fischer (New York: Oxford University Press, 2016), 30–47.

Budolfson, Mark, "Consumer Ethics, Harm Footprints, and the Empirical Dimensions of Food Choices," in *Philosophy Comes to Dinner: Arguments about the Ethics of Eating* (New York: Routledge, 2016a), 163–181.

Budolfson, Mark Bryant, "Is It Wrong to Eat Meat from Factory Farms? If So, Why?" in *The Moral Complexities of Eating Meat*, edited by Ben Bramble and Bob Fischer (New York: Oxford University Press, 2016b), 80–98.

Budolfson, Mark Bryant, "The Inefficacy Objection to Consequentialism and the Problem with the Expected Consequences Response," *Philosophical Studies* 176, no. 7 (2019): 1711–1724.

Buijs, Stephanie and Ramon Muns, "A Review of the Effects of Non-Straw Enrichment on Tail Biting in Pigs," *Animals* 9, no. 10 (2019): 824.

Burkholder, JoAnn, Bob Libra, Peter Weyer, Susan Heathcote, Dana Kolpin, Peter S. Thorne, and Michael Wichman, "Impacts of Waste from Concentrated Animal Feeding Operations on Water Quality," *Environmental Health Perspectives* 115, no. 2 (2007): 308–312.

Buzby, Jean C., Hodan Farah Wells, Bruce Axtman, and Jana Mickey, "Supermarket Loss Estimates for Fresh Fruit, Vegetables, Meat, Poultry, and Seafood and Their Use in the ERS Loss-Adjusted Food Availability Data," *USDA Economic Information Bulletin* 44 (2009).

Buzby, Jean C., Jeanine T. Bentley, Beth Padera, Jennifer Campuzano, and Cara Ammon, "Updated Supermarket Shrink Estimates for Fresh Foods and Their Implications for ERS Loss-Adjusted Food Availability Data," *USDA Economic Information Bulletin* 155 (2016).

Callicott, J. Baird, "Animal Liberation: A Triangular Affair," *Environmental Ethics* 2, no. 4 (1980): 311–338.

Calhoun, Cheshire, "Standing for Something," *The Journal of Philosophy* 92, no. 5 (1995): 235–260.

Campbell, Joy M., Joe D. Crenshaw, and Javier Polo, "The Biological Stress of Early Weaned Piglets," *Journal of Animal Science and Biotechnology* 4 (2013), art. 19.

Campbell, T. Colin and Thomas M. Campbell II, *The China Study, Revised and Expanded Edition* (Dallas: BenBella Books, 2016).

Carruthers, Peter, *The Animals Issue* (New York: Cambridge University Press, 1992).

Centers for Disease Control and Prevention, "2009 H1N1 Pandemic (H1N1pdm09 virus)" (2019), available online at https://www.cdc.gov/flu/pandemic-resources/2009-h1n1-pandemic.html.

Centers for Disease Control, "COVID-19 Among Workers in Meat and Poultry Processing Facilities—United States, April–May 2020," *Morbidity and Mortality Weekly Report* 69, no. 27 (2020): 887–892.

Chartier, Gary, "On the Threshold Argument against Consumer Meat Purchases," *Journal of Social Philosophy* 37, no. 2 (2006): 233–249.

Clauer, Philip, "Modern Meat Chicken Industry," *Penn State Extension* (2012), available online at https://extension.psu.edu/modern-meat-chicken-industry.

Consumer Reports National Research Center, *Food Labels Survey: 2016 Nationally-Representative Phone Survey* (Washington, DC: Consumer Reports, 2016).

Cuneo, Terence, "Conscientious Omnivorism," in *Philosophy Comes to Dinner: Arguments about the Ethics of Eating*, edited by Andrew Chignell, Terence Cuneo, and Matthew C. Halteman (New York: Routledge, 2016), 21–38.

Cunningham, Dan L., "Nuisance Myths and Poultry Farming," in *Learning for Life Bulletin* 1299 (Athens, GA: University of Georgia Extension, 2012).

Davis, Steven L., "The Least Harm Principle May Require that Humans Consume a Diet Containing Large Herbivores, Not a Vegan Diet," *Journal of Agricultural and Environmental Ethics* 16, no. 4 (2003): 387–394.

DeGrazia, David, "Moral Vegetarianism from a Very Broad Base," *Journal of Moral Philosophy* 6, no. 2 (2009): 143–165.

De Jong, I.C. and D. Guémené, "Major Welfare Issues in Broiler Breeders," *World's Poultry Science Journal* 67, no. 1 (2011): 73–82.

Devine, Philip E., "The Moral Basis of Vegetarianism," *Philosophy* 53, no. 206 (1978): 481–505.

Diamond, Cora, "Eating Animals and Eating People," *Philosophy* 53, no. 20 (1978): 465–479.

Dombrowski, Daniel A., *Babies and Beasts: The Argument from Marginal Cases* (Urbana, IL: University of Illinois Press, 1997).

Donham, Kelley J., Debra Cumro, and Steve Reynolds, "Synergistic Effects of Dust and Ammonia on the Occupational Health Effects of Poultry Production Worlers," *Journal of Agromedicine* 8, no. 2 (2002): 57–76.

Driver, Julia, "Individual Consumption and Moral Complicity," in *The Moral Complexities of Eating Meat*, edited by Bob Fischer and Ben Bramble (Oxford University Press, 2016), 67–79.

Earle, Megan and Gordon Hodson, "What's Your Beef with Vegetarians? Predicting Anti-Vegetarian Prejudice from Pro-Beef Attitudes across Cultures," *Personality and Individual Differences* 119 (2017): 52–55.

EFSA Panel on Animal Health and Welfare, "Scientific Opinion Concerning the Welfare of Animals during Transport," *EFSA Journal* 9, no. 1 (2011): art. 1966.

EFSA Panel on Animal Health and Welfare, "Slaughter of Animals: Poultry," *EFSA Journal* 17, no. 11 (2019a): art. 5849.

EFSA Panel on Animal Health and Welfare, "Killing for Purposes Other than Slaughter: Poultry," *EFSA Journal* 17, no. 11 (2019b): art. 5850.

Egonsson, Dan, "Kant's Vegetarianism," *Journal of Value Inquiry* 31 (1997): 473–483, at 473–477.

Engel, Mylan, "The Commonsense Case for Ethical Vegetarianism," *Between the Species* 19, no. 1 (2016): 2–31.

Everett, Jennifer, "Environmental Ethics, Animal Welfarism, and the Problem of Predation: A Bambi Lover's Respect for Nature," *Ethics & the Environment* 6, no. 1 (2001): 42–67.

Fairlie, Simon, *Meat: A Benign Extravagance* (White River Junction, VT: Chelsea Green, 2010).

Fischer, Bob, *The Ethics of Eating Meat: Usually Bad, Sometimes Wrong, Often Permissible* (New York: Routledge, 2020).

Foer, Jonathan Safran, *Eating Animals* (New York: Little, Brown & Co., 2009).

Francione, Gary, *Introduction to Animal Rights: Your Child or the Dog* (Philadelphia: Temple University Press, 2000).

Fraser, D., "Observations on the Behavioural Development of Suckling and Early-Weaned Piglets during the First Six Weeks after Birth," *Animal Behaviour* 26, no. 1 (1978): 22–30.

Fraser, David, "Understanding Animal Welfare," *Acta Veterinaria Scandinavica* 50 (2008): S1.

Freiman, Christopher, *Why It's OK to Ignore Politics* (New York: Routledge, 2021).

Frey, Raymond G., "Moral Standing, the Value of Lives, and Speciesism," *Between the Species* 4, no. 3 (1988): 191–201.

Garrett, Jeremy R., "Utilitarianism, Vegetarianism, and Human Health: A Response to the Causal Impotence Objection," *Journal of Applied Philosophy* 24, no. 3 (2007): 223–237.

Gaus, Gerald F., *On Philosophy, Politics, and Economics* (Belmont, CA: Thomson Wadsworth, 2008).

Gerber, J., H. Steinfeld, B. Henderson, A. Mottet, C. Opio, J. Dikman, A. Falcucci, and G. Tempio, *Tackling Climate Change through Livestock: A Global Assessment of Emissions and Mitigation Opportunities* (Rome: Food and Agriculture Organization of the United Nations, 2013).

Global Animal Partnership, *Global Animal Partnership's 5-Step Animal Welfare Rating Standards for Chickens Raised for Meat v3.1* (Austin, TX: Global Animal Partnership, 2017).

Global Animal Partnership, *Global Animal Partnership's 5-Step Animal Welfare Standards for Pigs v2.4* (Austin, TX: Global Animal Partnership, 2020).

Global Animal Partnership, "For Producers" (2021a), available online at https://globalanimalpartnership.org/producers/.

Global Animal Partnership, "For Shoppers" (2021b), available online at https://globalanimalpartnership.org/shoppers/.

Global Institute of Sustainable Forestry, "Cattle Ranching in the Amazon Region," *Global Forest Atlas* (2020), available online at https://globalforestatlas.yale.edu/amazon/land-use/cattle-ranching.

Grandin, Temple and Benjamin Hale, "An Interview with Temple Grandin," *Conjunctions* 61 (2013): 109–119.

Graves, H.B., "Behavior and Ecology of Wild and Feral Swine (Sus scrofa)," *Journal of Animal Science* 58, no. 2 (1984): 482–492.

Gruen, Lori, *Ethics and Animals: An Introduction* (New York: Cambridge University Press, 2011).

Hemsworth, P.H., "Key Determinants of Pig Welfare: Implications of Animal Management and Housing Design on Livestock Welfare," *Animal Production Science* 58, no. 8 (2018): 1375–1386.

Hemsworth, P.H., J.L. Barnett, C. Hansen, and C.G. Winfield, "Effects of Social Environment on Welfare Status and Sexual Behaviour of Female Pigs II: Effects of Space Allowance," *Applied Animal Behaviour Science* 16, no. 3 (1986): 259–267.

Hill, Thomas E. Jr., "Ideals of Human Excellence and Preserving Natural Environments," *Environmental Ethics* 5, no. 3 (1983): 211–224.

Hooker, Brad, *Ideal Code, Real World: A Rule-Consequentialist Theory of Morality* (New York: Oxford University Press, 2000).

Horta, Oscar, "The Scope of the Argument from Species Overlap," *Journal of Applied Philosophy* 31, no. 2 (2014): 142–154.

Huemer, Michael, *Dialogues on Ethical Vegetarianism* (New York: Routledge, 2019).

Human Rights Watch, *Blood, Sweat, and Fear: Workers' Rights in U.S. Meat and Poultry Plants* (New York: Human Rights Watch, 2004).

Human Rights Watch, *"When We're Dead and Buried, Our Bones Will Keep Hurting": Workers' Rights Under Threat in US Meat and Poultry Plants* (New York: Human Rights Watch, 2019).

Humane Farm Animal Care, *Humane Farm Animal Care Animal Care Standards, August 2014: Chickens* (Middleburg, VA: Humane Farm Animal Care, 2018a).

Humane Farm Animal Care, *Humane Farm Animal Care Animal Care Standards, January 2018: Pigs* (Middleburg, VA: Humane Farm Animal Care, 2018b).

Humane Farm Animal Care, "Producers who are Certified Humane" (2021), available online at https://certifiedhumane.org/whos-certified-2/.

Humane Research Council, "Study of Current and Former Vegetarians and Vegans" (2014), available online at https://faunalytics.org/wp-content/uploads/2015/06/Faunalytics_Current-Former-Vegetarians_Full-Report.pdf.

Humane Society of the United States, "Welfare Issues with the Transport of Day-Old Chicks" (2008), available online at https://www.humanesociety.org/sites/default/files/docs/hsus-report-chick-transport-welfiss.pdf.

Jacobs, Leonie, Evelyn Delezie, Luc Duchateau, Klara Goethals, and Frank A.M. Tuyttens, "Impact of the Separate Pre-slaughter Stages on Broiler Chicken Welfare," *Poultry Science* 96, no. 2 (2017): 266–273.

Jacobson, Daniel, "Fitting Attitude Theories of Value," *Stanford Encyclopedia of Philosophy* (2011), available online at https://plato.stanford.edu/entries/fitting-attitude-theories/.

Kagan, Shelly, "Do I Make a Difference?" *Philosophy & Public Affairs* 39, no. 2 (2011): 105–141.

Kant, Immanuel, *Groundwork of the Metaphysics of Morals*, translated and edited by Mary Gregor (New York: Cambridge University Press, [1785] 2006).

Kittay, Eva Feder, "The Personal Is Philosophical Is Political: A Philosopher and Mother of a Cognitively Disabled Person Sends Notes from the Battlefield," *Metaphilosophy* 40, nos. 3–4 (2009): 606–627.

Kluger, Jeffrey, "Sorry Vegans: Here's How Meat-Eating Made Us Human," *TIME* (2016), available online at https://time.com/4252373/meat-eating-veganism-evolution/.

Korsgaard, Christine, *Fellow Creatures: Our Obligations to the Other Animals* (New York: Oxford University Press, 2018).

Lamey, Andy, "The Animal Ethics of Temple Grandin: A Protectionist Analysis," *Journal of Agricultural and Environmental Ethics* 32, no. 1 (2019): 143–164.

Lenhart, Steven W., Peter D. Morris, Robert E. Akin, Stephen A. Olenchock, William S. Service, and William P. Boone, "Organic Dust, Endotoxin, and Ammonia Exposures in the North Carolina Poultry Processing Industry," *Applied Occupational and Environmental Hygiene* 5, no. 9 (1990): 611–618.

Lestel, Dominique, *Eat This Book: A Carnivore's Manifesto* (New York: Columbia University Press, 2016).

Levy, Neil, "Vegetarianism: Toward Ideological Impurity," in *The Moral Complexities of Eating Meat*, edited by Ben Bramble and Bob Fischer (New York: Oxford University Press, 2016), 172–184.

Lewis, Hannah C., Kåre Mølbak, Catrin Reese, Frank M. Aarestrup, Mette Selchau, Marit Sørum, and Robert L. Skov, "Pigs as Source of Methicillin-Resistant *Staphylococcus aureus* CC398 Infections in Humans, Denmark," *Emerging Infectious Diseases* 14, no. 9 (2008): 1383–1389.

Lindemann Nelson, Hilde, "What Child Is This?" *Hastings Center Report* 32, no. 6 (2002): 29–38.

Linzey, Andrew, *Animal Theology* (Urbana, IL: University of Illinois Press, 1994).

Lomasky, Loren, *Persons, Rights, and the Moral Community* (New York: Oxford University Press, 1987).

Lomasky, Loren, "Is It Wrong to Eat Animals?" *Social Philosophy & Policy* 30, nos. 1–2 (2013): 177–200.

MacDonald, James M., *Technology, Organization, and Financial Performance in U.S. Broiler Production* (Washington, DC: U.S. Department of Agriculture Economic Research Service, 2014).

MacInnis, Cara C. and Gordon Hodson, "It Ain't Easy Eating Greens: Evidence of Bias toward Vegetarians and Vegans from Both Source and Target," *Group Processes & Intergroup Relations* 20, no. 6 (2017): 721–744.

MacLean, Douglas, "Is 'Human Being' a Moral Concept?" *Philosophy & Public Policy Quarterly* 30, nos. 3–4 (2010): 16–20.

Mallin, Michael A. and Lawrence B. Cahoon, "Industrialized Animal Production—A Major Source of Nutrient and Microbial Pollution to Aquatic Ecosystems," *Population and Environment* 24, no. 5 (2003): 369–385.

Marchant-Forde, Jeremy N., *Sow Welfare Fact Sheet: Housing and Welfare of Sows during Gestation* (West Lafayette, IN: USDA Agricultural Research Service, 2010).

Marchant-Forde, Jeremy N., *Swine Welfare Fact Sheet: Welfare of Sows and Piglets at Farrowing* (West Lafayette, IN: USDA Agricultural Research Service, 2011).

Markowski, Kelly L. and Susan Roxburgh, "'If I Became a Vegan, My Family and Friends Would Hate Me:' Anticipating Vegan Stigma as a Barrier to Plant-Based Diets," *Appetite* 135 (2019): 1–9.

Mayo Clinic Staff, "How Meat and Poultry Fit in Your Healthy Diet," *Healthy Lifestyle: Nutrition and Healthy Eating* (2019), available online at https://www.mayoclinic.org/healthy-lifestyle/nutrition-and-healthy-eating/in-depth/food-and-nutrition/art-20048095.

Mayo Clinic Staff, "Vegetarian Diet: How to Get the Best Nutrition," *Healthy Lifestyle: Nutrition and Healthy Eating* (2020), available online at https://www.mayoclinic.org/healthy-lifestyle/nutrition-and-healthy-eating/in-depth/vegetarian-diet/art-20046446.

McBride, William D. and Kenneth Mathews Jr., *The Diverse Structure and Organization of U.S. Beef Cow-Calf Farms* (Washington, DC: USDA Economic Research Service, 2011).

McBride, William D. and Nigel Key, *US Hog Production from 1992 to 2009: Technology, Restructuring, and Productivity Growth* (Washington, DC: U.S. Department of Agriculture, 2013).

McGlone, John J. and Mhairi Sutherland, "Is Tail Docking Necessary and, If So, How Long Should the Tail Be?" in *Pork Checkoff Research Report: Animal Welfare* NPB #06-183 (Des Moines, IA: National Pork Board, 2009).

McMahan, Jeff, *The Ethics of Killing: Problems at the Margins of Life* (New York: Oxford University Press, 2002).

McMahan, Jeff, "Eating Animals the Nice Way," *Dædalus* 137, no. 1 (2008): 66–76.

McMahan, Jeff, "The Moral Problem of Predation," in *Philosophy Comes to Dinner: Arguments about the Ethics of Eating*, edited by Andrew Chignell, Terence Cuneo, Matthew C. Halteman (New York: Routledge, 2016), 268–293.

McMurray, Bryan, "Cow Size Is Growing," *Beef Magazine* (Feb. 1, 2009), available online at https://www.beefmagazine.com/genetics/0201-increased-beef-cows.

McPherson, Tristram, "Why I Am a Vegan (and You Should Be One Too)," in *Philosophy Comes to Dinner: Arguments about the Ethics of Eating*, edited by

Andrew Chignell, Terence Cuneo, and Matthew C. Halteman (New York: Routledge, 2016), 73–91.

Mill, John Stuart, "On Nature," in *Nature, the Utility of Religion, and Theism* (London: Longmans, Green & Co., [1874] 1885), 3–65.

Mirabelli, Maria C., Steve Wing, Stephen W. Marshall, and Timothy C. Wilcosky, "Asthma Symptoms among Adolescents Who Attend Public Schools that are Located Near Confined Swine Feeding Operations," *Pediatrics* 118, no. 1 (2006): e66–e75.

Montgomery, Sy, *Temple Grandin: How the Girl Who Loved Cows Embraced Autism and Changed the World* (Boston: Houghton Mifflin Harcourt, 2012).

Nagaraja, T.G. and Kelly F. Lechtenberg, "Acidosis in Feedlot Cattle," *Veterinary Clinics of North America: Food Animal Practice* 23, no. 2 (2007): 333–350.

National Cattlemen's Beef Association, *Beef Quality Assurance: National Manual* (Centennial, CO: National Cattlemen's Beef Association, 2019).

National Chicken Council, *National Chicken Council Animal Welfare Guidelines and Audit Checklist for Broilers* (Washington, DC: National Chicken Council, 2019a).

National Chicken Council, "Questions and Answers about Antibiotics in Chicken Production" (2019b), available online at https://www.national-chickencouncil.org/questions-answers-antibiotics-chicken-production/.

National Chicken Council, "Broiler Chicken Industry Key Facts 2020" (2021a), available online at https://www.nationalchickencouncil.org/statistic/broiler-industry-key-facts/.

National Chicken Council, "Processing: How Are Chickens Slaughtered and Processed for Meat?" *Chicken Check In* (2021b), available online at https://www.chickencheck.in/faq/how-chickens-slaughtered-processed/.

National Chicken Council, "U.S. Broiler Performance: 1925 to Present" (2021c), available online at https://www.nationalchickencouncil.org/statistic/us-broiler-performance/.

National Pork Board, *Common Swine Industry Audit: Instructions, Standards, and Audit Tool* (Des Moines, IA: National Pork Board, 2021).

Nefsky, Julia, "Consequentialism and the Problem of Collective Harm: A Reply to Kagan," *Philosophy & Public Affairs* 39, no. 4 (2011): 364–395.

Nefsky, Julia, "How You Can Help, Without Making A Difference," *Philosophical Studies* 174, no. 11 (2017): 2743–2767.

Nicol, C.J. and G.B. Scott, "Pre-slaughter Handling and Transport of Broiler Chickens," *Applied Animal Behaviour Science* 28, nos. 1–2 (1990): 57–73.

Neilsen Retail Measurement Services, "Meet the New 'Meat' Eater" (Aug. 5, 2019), available online at https://www.nielsen.com/us/en/insights/article/2019/meet-the-new-meat-eater/.

Norcross, Alastair, "Puppies, Pigs, and People: Eating Meat and Marginal Cases," *Philosophical Perspectives* 18 (2004): 229–245.

North American Meat Institute, "Video Tour of a Beef Plant featuring Temple Grandin" (2012), available online at https://www.youtube.com/watch?v=VMqYYXswono.

North American Meat Institute, "Video Tour of a Pork Plant featuring Temple Grandin" (2013), available online at https://www.youtube.com/watch?v=LsEbvwMipJI.

North American Meat Institute, *Recommended Animal Handling Guidelines & Audit Guide: A Systematic Approach to Animal Welfare* (Washington, DC: North American Meat Institute, 2019).

Norwood, Bailey F. and Jason F. Lusk, *Compassion, by the Pound: The Economics of Farm Animal Welfare* (New York: Oxford University Press, 2011).

O'Connell, N.E. and V.E. Beattie, "Influence of Environmental Enrichment on Aggressive Behaviour and Dominance Relationships in Growing Pigs," *Animal Welfare* 8, no. 3 (1999): 269–279.

OpenSecrets, "Livestock" (2021a), available online at https://www.opensecrets.org/industries/indus.php?ind=A06++.

OpenSecrets, "Meat Processing & Products" (2021b), available online at https://www.opensecrets.org/industries/indus.php?ind=G2300.

OpenSecrets, "Poultry & Eggs" (2021c), available online at https://www.opensecrets.org/industries/indus.php?ind=A05++.

Origen, *On First Principles* (New York: Harper & Row, 1966).

Ottolenghi, Yotam, *Plenty* (San Francisco: Chronicle Books, 2011).

PaleoLeap, "How Vegetarianism Is Bad For You and the Environment," *PaleoLeap* (2020), available online at https://paleoleap.com/vegetarianism-bad-environment/.

Palmer, Clare, *Animal Ethics in Context* (New York: Columbia University Press, 2010).

Pearce, G.P. and A.M. Paterson, "The Effect of Space Restriction and Provision of Toys during Rearing on the Behaviour, Productivity, and Physiology of Male Pigs," *Applied Animal Behaviour Science* 36, no. 1 (1993): 11–28.

Perdue Foods, "Programs and Practices" (2021), available online at https://corporate.perduefarms.com/responsibility/animal-care/programs-practices/.

Pfeiler, Tamara M. and Boris Egloff, "Do Vegetarians Feel Bad? Examining the Association between Eating Vegetarian and Subjective Well-Being in Two Representative Samples," *Food Quality and Preference* 86 (2020): art. 104018.

Philo of Alexandria, *Philo in Ten Volumes, and Two Supplementary Volumes* (Cambridge, MA: Harvard University Press, 1929–1962).

Bibliography

Pilgrim's Pride, "Environment" (2020), available online at https://sustainability.pilgrims.com/chapters/environment/.

Pinker, Steven, *The Better Angels of Our Nature: Why Violence Has Declined* (New York: Viking Books, 2011).

Plato, "Gorgias," in *Plato: Complete Works*, edited by John M. Cooper (Indianapolis, IN: Hackett Publishing Co., 1997), 791–869.

Plumwood, Val, "Being Prey," *Terra Nova* 1, no. 3 (1996): 32–44.

Pollan, Michael, *The Omnivore's Dilemma: A Natural History of Four Meals* (New York: Penguin Books, 2006).

Pork Checkoff, "Life Cycle of a Market Pig" (2016), available online at https://www.pork.org/facts/pig-farming/life-cycle-of-a-market-pig/.

Professional Animal Auditor Certification Organization, "Leadership: Founding Members, Board of Directors, Committees & Staff" (2021), available online at https://animalauditor.org/About/Members.

Purves, Duncan and Nicolas Delon, in "Meaning in the Lives of Humans and Other Animals," *Philosophical Studies* 175, no. 2 (2018): 317–338.

Raterman, Ty, "An Environmentalist's Lament of Predation," *Environmental Ethics* 30, no. 4 (2008): 417–434.

Raterman, Ty, "Bearing the Weight of the World: On the Extent of an Individual's Environmental Responsibility," *Environmental Values* 21, no. 4 (2012): 417–436.

Rawls, John, "Two Concepts of Rules," *The Philosophical Review* 64, no. 1 (1955): 3–32.

Rawls, John, *A Theory of Justice, Revised Edition* (Cambridge, MA: Harvard University Press, 1999).

Regan, Tom, *The Case for Animal Rights* (Berkeley, CA: University of California Press, 1987).

Ritchie, Hannah and Max Roser, "Meat and Dairy Production," *Our World in Data* (2019), available online at https://ourworldindata.org/meat-production.

Rosenthal, Benjamin M., Guiseppe LaRosa, Dante Zarlenga, Detiger Dunams, Yao Chunyu, Liu Mingyuan, and Edoardo Pozio, "Human Dispersal of *Trichinella spiralis* in Domesticated Pigs," *Infection, Genetics and Evolution* 8, no. 6 (2008): 799–805.

Rousseau, Jean-Jacques, *Discourse on the Origin of Inequality*, translated by Donald A. Cress (Indianapolis, IN: Hackett Publishing, 1992).

Ruff, Michael D., "Important Parasites in Poultry Production Systems," *Veterinary Parasitology* 84, nos. 3–4 (1999): 337–347.

Rutherford, Burt, "The Calf-Fed Conundrum," *Beef Magazine* (Jan. 30, 2019), available online at https://www.beefmagazine.com/commentary/calf-fed-conundrum.

Ryder, Richard, "Speciesism Again: The Original Leaflet," *Critical Society* 2 (2010).

Sagoff, Mark, "Animal Liberation and Environmental Ethics: Bad Marriage, Quick Divorce," *Osgoode Hall Law Journal* 22, no. 2 (1984): 297–307.

SalaryExpert, "Chicken Catcher Salary" (2021a), available online at https://www.salaryexpert.com/salary/job/chicken-catcher/united-states.

SalaryExpert, "Slaughter Laborer" (2021b), available online at https://www.salaryexpert.com/salary/job/slaughter-laborer/united-states.

Schmidtz, David, "Natural Enemies: An Anatomy of Environmental Conflict," *Environmental Ethics* 22, no. 4 (2000): 397–408.

Scully, Matthew, *Dominion: The Power of Man, the Suffering of Animals, and the Call to Mercy* (New York: St. Martin's Press, 2002).

Shafer-Landau, Russ, "Vegetarianism, Causation and Ethical Theory," *Public Affairs Quarterly* 8, no. 1 (1994): 85–100.

Shafer-Landau, Russ, *Living Ethics: An Introduction with Readings* (New York: Oxford University Press, 2019).

Šimčikas, Saulius, "Is the Percentage of Vegetarians and Vegans in the U.S. Increasing?" *Animal Charity Evaluators* (2018), available online at https://animalcharityevaluators.org/blog/is-the-percentage-of-vegetarians-and-vegans-in-the-u-s-increasing/.

Singer, Peter, "All Animals are Equal," *Philosophic Exchange* 5, no. 1 (1974): 103–116.

Singer, Peter, "Utilitarianism and Vegetarianism," *Philosophy & Public Affairs* 9, no. 4 (1980): 325–337.

Singer, Peter, *Animal Liberation, Updated Edition* (New York: HarperCollins, 2009).

Singer, Peter, *Practical Ethics, Third Edition* (New York: Cambridge University Press, 2011).

Stolba, A. and D.G.M. Wood-Gush, "The Identification of Behavioural Key Features and their Incorporation into a Housing Design for Pigs," *Annales de Recherches Vétérinaires* 15, no. 2 (1984): 287–302.

Taylor, K.C., "Automobile Catalytic Converters," *Studies in Surface Science and Catalysis* 30 (1987): 97–116.

Temple, D., E. Mainau, and X. Manteca, "Tail Biting in Pigs," *The Farm Animal Welfare Fact Sheet* 8 (2014), available online at https://www.fawec.org/media/com_lazypdf/pdf/fs8-en.pdf.

Thompson, Paul B., "Philosophical Ethics and the Improvement of Farmed Animal Lives," *Animal Frontiers* 10, no. 1 (2020): 21–28.

Tonsor, Glynn and Robin Reid, "Livestock Budgets," *AgManager.info* (2020), available online at https://www.agmanager.info/farm-mgmt-guides/livestock-budgets.

Tyson Foods, "Environment: Summary Overview" (2020), available online at https://www.tysonsustainability.com/environment/.

U.S. Department of Agriculture, "Defend the Flock Program" (2021), available online at https://www.aphis.usda.gov/aphis/ourfocus/animalhealth/animal-disease-information/avian/defend-the-flock-program.

U.S. Department of Agriculture Economic Research Service, "Cattle & Beef: Sector at a Glance" (2020), available online at https://www.ers.usda.gov/topics/animal-products/cattle-beef/sector-at-a-glance/.

U.S. Department of Agriculture National Agricultural Statistics Service, "Agriculture Counts: Cattle" (Jan. 2021a), available online at https://www.nass.usda.gov/Publications/Todays_Reports/reports/catl0121.pdf.

U.S. Department of Agriculture National Agricultural Statistics Service, "Quarterly Hogs and Pigs" (Mar. 2021b), available online at https://downloads.usda.library.cornell.edu/usda-esmis/files/rj430453j/7p88db205/mw22w1890/hgpg0321.pdf.

U.S. Environmental Protection Agency, "National Air Emissions Monitoring Study" (2020a), available online at https://www.epa.gov/afos-air/national-air-emissions-monitoring-study.

U.S. Environmental Protection Agency, "National Pollutant Discharge Elimination System (NPDES): Animal Feeding Operations (AFOs)," (2020b), available online at https://www.epa.gov/npdes/animal-feeding-operations-afos.

U.S. Environmental Protection Agency, "Estimated Animal Agriculture Nitrogen and Phosphorus from Manure" (2021), available online at https://www.epa.gov/nutrient-policy-data/estimated-animal-agriculture-nitrogen-and-phosphorus-manure.

Warfield, Ted A., "Eating Dead Animals: Meat Eating, Meat Purchasing, and Proving Too Much," in Philosophy Comes to Dinner: Arguments about the Ethics of Eating, edited by Andrew Chignell, Terence Cuneo, and Matthew C. Halteman (New York: Routledge, 2016), 151–162.

WATTPoultryUSA, "2021 Top Poultry Companies" (March 2021), p. 21, available online at https://www.wattpoultryusa-digital.com/wattpoultryusa/march_2021/.

Williams, Bernard, "The Human Prejudice," in Philosophy as a Humanistic Discipline (Princeton, NJ: Princeton University Press, 2006), 135–152.

Williams, R.M., "On the Tail-Docking of Pigs, Human Circumcision, and Their Implications for Prevailing Opinion Regarding Pain," Journal of Applied Philosophy 20, no. 1 (2003): 89–93.

Wing, Steve, Rachel Avery Horton, Stephen W. Marshall, Kendall Thu, Mansoureh Tajik, Leah Schinasi, and Susan S. Schiffman, "Air Pollution and Odor in Communities Near Industrial Swine Operations," Environmental Health Perspectives 116, no. 10 (2008): 1362–1368.

Widowski, Tina and Stephanie Torrey, "Neonatal Management Practices," *Swine Welfare Fact Sheet* 1, no. 6 (Des Moines, IA: National Pork Board, 2002).

Wolk, A., "Potential Health Hazards of Eating Red Meat," *Journal of Internal Medicine* 281, no. 2 (2017): 106–122.

Zaraska, Marta, "Meeting Meat-Eaters Halfway: Why Reducetarianism Works Better Than Moralizing," *Breakthrough Journal* 10 (2019), available online at https://thebreakthrough.org/journal/no-10-winter-2019/meeting-meat-eaters-halfway.

Index

Printed in Great Britain
by Amazon

24641563R00136